T0339475

Heidegger and Entrepreneurship

This book proposes that entrepreneurial practice is often considered an "applicable" paradigm—an "applicable" paradigm, which focuses too much on planned, analytical, calculable, tool-based and ready-to-hand modes of decision-making action. Hence, the equally important "theory of Nothing" has not received the attention it deserves.

With reference to Heidegger's existence-oriented philosophy, *Heidegger and Entrepreneurship: A Phenomenological Approach* indicates how nothing can be a condition for an entrepreneurial applicable paradigm. It is suggested that the "theory of Nothing" bears the possibility of further development and can re-create the entrepreneurial paradigm of applying and decision-making. This may also indicate a structure for understanding the new possibilities in entrepreneurship practice, such as entrepreneurial education and research. The book will be of value to students, researchers and academics with an interest in entrepreneurship, management and innovation.

Håvard Åsvoll is Associate Professor of Organization and Management at the Faculty of Social Sciences at Nord University, Norway.

Routledge Focus on Business and Management

The fields of business and management have grown exponentially as areas of research and education. This growth presents challenges for readers trying to keep up with the latest important insights. Routledge Focus on Business and Management presents small books on big topics and how they intersect with the world of business research.

Individually, each title in the series provides coverage of a key academic topic, whilst collectively, the series forms a comprehensive collection across the business disciplines.

How to Resolve Conflict in Organizations
The Power of People Models and Procedure
Annamaria Garden

Branding and Positioning in Base of Pyramid Markets in Africa
Innovative Approaches
Charles Blankson, Stanley Coffie and Joseph Darmoe

Persuasion
The Hidden Forces that Influence Negotiations
Jasper Kim

The Neuroscience of Rhetoric in Management
Compassionate Executive Communication
Dirk Remley

Heidegger and Entrepreneurship
A Phenomenological Approach
Håvard Åsvoll

For more information about this series, please visit: www.routledge.com/ Routledge-Focus-on-Business-and-Management/book-series/FBM

Heidegger and Entrepreneurship

A Phenomenological Approach

Håvard Åsvoll

Routledge
Taylor & Francis Group

NEW YORK AND LONDON

First published 2019
by Routledge
605 Third Avenue, New York, NY 10017

and by Routledge
2 Park Square, Milton Park, Abingdon, Oxon, OX14 4RN

First issued in paperback 2021

Routledge is an imprint of the Taylor & Francis Group, an informa business

Copyright © 2019 Taylor & Francis

The right of Håvard Åsvoll to be identified as author of this work has been asserted by him in accordance with sections 77 and 78 of the Copyright, Designs and Patents Act 1988.

All rights reserved. No part of this book may be reprinted or reproduced or utilized in any form or by any electronic, mechanical, or other means, now known or hereafter invented, including photocopying and recording, or in any information storage or retrieval system, without permission in writing from the publishers.

Trademark notice: Product or corporate names may be trademarks or registered trademarks, and are used only for identification and explanation without intent to infringe.

Publisher's Note
The publisher has gone to great lengths to ensure the quality of this reprint but points out that some imperfections in the original copies may be apparent.

Library of Congress Cataloging-in-Publication Data
Names: Asvoll, Havard, author.
Title: Heidegger and entrepreneurship : a phenomenological approach / Havard Asvoll.
Description: New York, NY : Routledge, 2019. | Series: Routledge focus on business and management | Includes index.
Identifiers: LCCN 2018036718 | ISBN 9781138364776 (hardback) | ISBN 9780429431142 (ebook)
Subjects: LCSH: Heidegger, Martin, 1889–1976. | Entrepreneurship— Philosophy.
Classification: LCC HB615 .A867 2019 | DDC 338/.0401—dc23
LC record available at https://lccn.loc.gov/2018036718

ISBN 13: 978-1-03-224177-7 (pbk)
ISBN 13: 978-1-138-36477-6 (hbk)

DOI: 10.4324/9780429431142

Typeset in Times New Roman
by Apex CoVantage, LLC

Contents

1 Introduction

In a very general way, the key framing of "Nothing" might be described as the loss of a common shared world of meaning, that is, the loss of a common home and the uncanny feeling. Behind the questions "What should I do?", "Where am I going?", and "How should I organize my business?", which are often being asked by entrepreneurs, fundamental questions might be hidden, such as "Who do I want to be?", "What am I?", and "Where is my home?" Ordinarily, entrepreneurs are at home in an organized everyday world. It is the feeling of being at home in such a familiar world that is suspended in the experience of Nothing. Ordinary equipment looks strange, everyday business activities pointless, and common-sense objectives outlandish. Entrepreneurs encountering "nothingness" feel uncanny and dislodged in a normal, familiar world. As this book might show, entrepreneurs with "Nothing" want to go home or to be at home at some point. In entrepreneurial practice, you might often say you have to come home because you think the situation is either too unsecure (lack of information) or risky or you search (diligently) for a new home in the sense of new life-projects and businesses. In this book, I will lay the ground for a further exploration of what entrepreneurs dwelling on "Nothing" mean when they express themselves in terms of "Nothing". What does "Nothing" mean to them?

When answering such questions, it is an advantage to know what we are looking for when we are talking about "Nothing". What, then, is the theory of nothing? What is the phenomenon of Nothing? And why do we need a theory of nothing especially with regard to entrepreneurially oriented research and practice? These are important questions, which this book seeks to answer. In order to do so it is necessary to provide a context or background for how Nothing may exist. Because Nothing exists, it is just a phenomenon not easily grasped and understood by entrepreneurs and researchers.

What, then, are the characteristics of an entrepreneurial context or background? One answer might be what is meant by an applicable paradigm in entrepreneurial research and practice. Or what is needed in entrepreneurship?

What does an entrepreneurial-student do? Of course, there are no clear-cut answers to these questions, but there seems to be some common challenges regarding decisions and how to apply tools concerning management, human resources and financial and market issues. Attached to this is the assumption that the entrepreneurial world rests on applicable equipment and decision-making, and that the entrepreneurial sciences and business of the sciences are about "preparing" for the best possible decisions, whether they be about opportunities, projects, pursuing careers, venture capitalists, or the decision-making process in general (Shepherd 2017). This, in short, also seems to be the justification for entrepreneurial education and business schools—there are decisions to be made, and we need to learn how to execute and handle them. A vast number of academic courses in entrepreneurship focus on the development of business plans and how they may be applicable under different circumstances. This involves the assembly of resources (knowledge) prior to the opportunity-exploration and opportunity-exploitation processes. From the view of the entrepreneurial-student, the emphasis is on decision-making tools and prelaunched strategies and experience of how the constituent parts of the venture creation, such as R&D, marketing, production and finance, are assembled and codified and are just waiting to be ordered (they are applicable). The entrepreneurial-student practice is characterized by the rational decision-making and planning (applicable) model that underpins the traditional entrepreneur and management models. Here it is possible to use a train metaphor; the knowledge and resources are ordered like railcars on a train, with a predictable and clear track laid out ahead. Once the train is assembled, the venture creation is initiated and can be implemented with a full head of steam. Such a metaphor may also be illuminating with regard to the applicable paradigm.

1.1   How May This "Applicable Paradigm" Look Like in Entrepreneurial Practice?

It seems like the business schools and institutes of entrepreneurship willingly adopt recent advancements in management/entrepreneurial tools and information systems. One of the main purposes is to increase the ability of entrepreneurial management students to progress towards optimal decision-making in their business plans and venture creation. Such logic can be said to rest on two cognitive constraints identified by Simon (1979): time (computational processing power) and memory (information storage and retrieval). Together with this decision-making approach, associated decision tools can be added, like the cost-benefit analysis, the SWOT analysis, and the net-present-value technique. Much of the academic status and legitimacy of business schools or institutes of entrepreneurship derives from the way in which they seem to signify commodified "decision-making knowledge" as well as the capacity to conduct decision-making in order to eventually create new ventures. A dominant and "trivializing" logic of reasoning seems to be that of resource utilization, the way in which a (student)-entrepreneur treats the world as a set of resources is a dominant logic of reasoning. This "commodified" or tool-based view in isolation may reduce decision-making to the (mechanical) application of preconceived rules for optimization. It may trivialize decision-making and makes it harder to show the entrepreneurs in pre-decision moments of a particular and unpredictable kind. And if this is a relevant description of how we understand entrepreneurial contexts, it makes it harder to discover and show the relevance of nothing and existence (potential of meaning). In Heideggerian terminology, the relevance of nothing may be said to be that it brings something to the light of day or lets things be. Nothing is there even if we cannot see it or articulate it, like a condition for our existence and the emergence or transformation of our self-understanding. Perhaps in one way, entrepreneurs can only be understood by existence and nothing, their way of living and dwelling in possibilities in the place (ethos). This implies a theoretical approach different from what underlies an applicable rational paradigm in entrepreneurship. Simply to "apply" something that is already there (i.e. analytical tools, practical techniques, formal procedures, and business plans) is to be able to assimilate it into an already existing and well-known category (the applicable paradigm), whilst being able to dwell in existence/nothing is being able to do something unique in a unique, never-before-encountered situation, i.e. to be able continually to do something for the first time. Thus, the resolution of an (experienced) Nothing is something manifested or displayed at a practical level in one's unique way of being *responsive* to the unique details of a situation by one's actual actions within it—not by categorizing it as an intellectual decision-making endeavour. This potential active responsiveness relies on one important condition, which might be called the passive synthesis of Nothing (more at 2.3). That is to say, during dwelling, entrepreneurs let themselves be enchanted into a (Nothing) movement with its own dynamics and aspects. Here, the significance of Nothing is neither the object nor the subject of Nothing but the temporary significance—Nothing as such.

Still influenced by the privileging in Descartes's philosophy of mind over body, active over passive, and thought over practical action, the applicable paradigm has tended to think of difficulties and problems as something to be solved by the application of rational thought and tools or ready-at-hand decision-making strategies. But as Heidegger (1962) makes clear, our being-in-the-world (and Nothing) is in many situations often of a much more practical than theoretical kind. Perhaps the entrepreneurial (research) practice is sometimes trapped in this Cartesian theoretical mode. If this is positive, we may develop a rational blindness to entrepreneurial practice. That is to say, maybe entrepreneurs and researchers also witness "Nothing" and potential disorientation, which have arisen out of preferring one form of knowledge and excluding others. We may have privileged applicable (ready-to-hand), orderly, theoretical knowledge and not paid so much attention to practical, emergent and situation-dependent aspects of knowledge. It is possible that a picture of a hidden order (reality as theory) behind appearances (practice) holds us captive. It is also possible that entrepreneurial research systematically (re)creates the objects (entrepreneur) of which it speaks. We draw meaning/knowledge of entrepreneurial practice from the embeddedness within an already pre-established order. Here, researchers' normative preferences are prevalent regarding the neo-classical "recognizer", the Kirznerian "discoverer" and Sarasvathy's claims about creative effectuation. Hence, the entrepreneur is framed and held captive as a rational (cognitive) opportunity man (i.e., Miller 2007) and decision-making creator (i.e., Sarasvathy, Dew, Velamuri, and Venkataraman 2003). This means that we may have inescapably entrapped ourselves/entrepreneurs within a whole way of looking at ourselves as consisting of "rational decision-makers", with "ready-to-hand tools" in (cognitive) motion according to established psychological laws, i.e. of seeing everything always as having had its beginnings in how we see things now. In short, the bold claim is that this rationalistic and applicable view of the world and of ourselves as consisting too much in configurations of self-contained, isolated parts (subject-object distinctions), applicable ready made all only linked together (if at all) by sets of abstract psychological (cognitive) laws and perspectives, is inadequate to how we in fact live our (entrepreneurial) lives. The message is: everything is ordered, just order! Even if it is analytical tools, practical techniques, formal procedures, implemented processes, business plans offered and used by entrepreneurs or pre-established theoretical/methodical perspectives and concepts chosen and facilitated by researchers. Here, the "orderability" and ready-to-hand mode of everything important is all-important.

In order to address such issues, this book is structured into three parts. Firstly, three assumptions of entrepreneurial theory and the potential of Nothing entrepreneurial theory are presented (2.1, 2.2, and 2.3). The thesis is that assumptions in entrepreneurial theory do not work for explaining phenomena of Nothing. Assumptions such as becoming, decision-making and activity are contrasted with Nothing companions like Being, being-in-the-world and passivity. The second part provides a description of how to move towards a theory of "Nothing" in entrepreneurial practice. This includes an introduction to Heidegger and the philosophy of Being and Nothing (3.1–3.6). Thereafter, vignettes and examples of entrepreneurial practice are presented on the basis of pivotal aspects of nothing (i.e. technology, projection and place) (4). This is followed by a model of nothing (consisting of main dimensions such as surfacing, embedding, sharing and resonance) trying to explicate where it might be possible for nothing to show up (5). The third part explains the implications of a theory of Nothing with regard to dominant entrepreneurial research, theory and education (6.1–6.3). At long last, entrepreneurship is framed as a new beginning (7). However, first, I describe the purpose of this book, and then I show how one might respond to Nothing (1.3). The last chapter before part 1 deals with Heidegger's philosophy in relation to entrepreneurial research (3.4).

1.2   The Purpose of This Book

I do not set out any theory (of nothing) or theoretical and fixed attitude towards practice in order to solve problems but look closely at what happens when Nothing shows itself. Perhaps the empirical examples have the effect of reminding us that in similar circumstances, we also can have similar detailed sensitivities. The examples and empirical material given work to highlight (entrepreneurs' and researchers') sensitive responses to Nothings in their surroundings or being-in-the-world.

Entrepreneurial studies seem reluctant to engage in "Nothing", or even related phenomena, such as absence, dangerous places, alienation, anomalies, fear, holes and gaps, lacks and losses, silences, impalpabilities and insipidities. Dominant paradigms and theories in entrepreneurship describe decision-making and how opportunities emerge and are recognized and discovered amidst incongruences (e.g., markets, customers, leadership and narratives), but the ability to describe how opportunities and decision-making may at first emerge and do not emerge from multiple possible and "impossible" Nothings (as possibilities) is lacking. This book tries to contribute to a perspective of how potential (Nothings) may come into entrepreneurial being and vice versa, in a constant being—nothing weaving. Furthermore, "Nothing" opens a new way of understanding how entrepreneurs are dependent on their context and existence. Inquiries into aspects of "Nothing" such as technology (applied paradigm), projection, and place may also help us to reframe the thinking about entrepreneurship or being entrepreneurial. Focusing on companions of "Nothing", that is, Being, being-in-the-world and passivity, serves to question pivotal assumptions in entrepreneurial research, theory and education. This book is written for those who sympathize with the spirit in which it is written. This is not, I believe, the spirit of the mainstream of entrepreneurship. The spirit of this entrepreneurship makes itself manifest in the technology (essence) of our time, in its innovations, opportunities and decisions, and it is uncongenial or uncanny to the author.

For Heidegger (1976/1993), the nothing is not nothing at all but, rather, does something: "the nothing itself noths or nihilates [das Nichts selbst nichtet]" (p. 140). This active "nothing" of the nothing both elicits and eludes complete conceptualization, a phenomenon we encounter when we go beyond our conception of what-is. To experience this "nothing" is to disclose something which is not a thing (hence "no-thing"). This informs our entrepreneurial and researching worlds as we experience primarily as what escapes or withdraws itself. This book points to such often forgotten and slippery but guiding (nothing) experiences, which in turn may challenge our (scientific) impulse to extend our conceptual mastery over entrepreneurial practice. In other words, this "nothing" can stand against (sometimes in a positive interweaving) the conceptual machinery of entrepreneurship (which I call the applicable paradigm). This is also an effort to not shy away from the significance of our emotional encounters with nothingness. They echo the groundlessness of human existence and any (ontic) discipline including entrepreneurship.

This book is not an effort to completely translate the sublime and often very difficult philosophical thinking of Heidegger into the realm of entrepreneurship studies or to enter into a difficult sorting out of the different periods and writings of Heidegger's thinking. There is no intention to offer a grand and novel theory of entrepreneurship or entrepreneurial life. Instead, I will show how some "forgotten" aspects and (nothing) possibilities in practice and in-between entrepreneurial practice, opportunities and decision-making/applicable paradigm. Even though I will talk of "a theory of Nothing", I do not claim to have such a theory. The way of thinking is to indicate that Being and nothingness show something beyond theory and language. "Nothing" is in fact beyond language, or, to be more precise, it tries to transgress the limits of language. This is a kind of phenomenology where the phenomena and subjectivity of human experience become more valued. Heidegger (1962) argues that much of the Western tradition has merely assumed a general theory about being human based on limited phenomena without adequately examining the phenomena themselves and without letting those phenomena guide any theorizing. In this sense, this book should be read as a prologue to a theory which does not yet exist and perhaps never will exist, because when it becomes fully blown and theoretically articulated, the theory will cease to exist. In other words, the recognition of Being can never be as clearly evident as theoretical recognition, and the quality of Nothing involves the abandonment of preconceived notions and logical puzzles. The Nothing denies the "is" of something. This phenomenology matches an interest in the experience as it unfolds. It is, in Heidegger's thinking (1962), not by means of conceptual analysis but through the (emotional) experience of Nothing that we can learn what we basically are as human beings, and hence how the nature of entrepreneurial practice could be understood. Therefore, in some sense, it seems we may be chosen being-there in order to explore the character of Nothing as the background out of which everything emerges. But there are different and more reserved answers to the question of how one might respond to nothing and the importance of being-there (Dasein).

1.3 How, Then, Does One Respond to Nothing?

As I see it, four initial possibilities present themselves: First, one can refuse to see (the problem of) nothing at all and continue as a pre-nothing researcher, entrepreneur, or metaphysician. You do not need to respond or are not capable; such is the temptation of both positivist science and entrepreneurial research (perhaps one of the dominant temptations in all research). Research embraces an anti-metaphysical quietism that wants to delineate the limits of philosophy from (entrepreneurial) research in order to clear a space of more on (psychological) cognitive, decision-making, and "opportunity" awaiting. Here, one can claim to have no metaphysical commitments and not to be concerned by not having them (the positivist attitude).This view would refuse to see the problem of nothing as an actual problem but see it simply as a symptom of a speculative metaphysical practice. It is possible to reject the "articulation potential" of Nothing on logical grounds (based on Wittgenstein's *Tractatus*).This interpretation refutes the value and meaning of Nothing being "transferred" in a satisfactory manner to an articulated language. A central and controversial statement about the interpretation of silence/Nothing is found in the last paragraph of Wittgenstein's (2005, paragraph 7.2) *Tractatus*: *Whereof one cannot speak, thereof one must be silent.* The main implication here is that silence/nothing must remain as nothing in scientific/philosophic language, and in colloquial language, because silence in art, music, literature, ethics and aesthetics is subject to transcendental conditions. That means, these aspects of life are impossible to formulate in words; they can only be indicated or shown in the ways we practice and live our lives. That is why it is impossible to achieve any articulated knowledge of silence and Nothingness, in life. Such an interpretation leaves a silent/ Nothing vocational practice to the practice itself, without the silence/ Nothingness having any meaning in any other contexts; e.g. researching silence/Nothingness within an entrepreneurial practice.

Second, one can react passively to nothing, accepting it as a trait or feeling of being, knowing the world to be uncanny, but also knowing that nothing one can do will change this. Such an experience of "nothing recession" may be linked to one interpretation of Wittgenstein's philosophy. This interpretation is not as reserved as the first with respect to whether a (nothing) practice can be expressed in other ways than simply through activities and the practice itself. One of the intentions of Wittgenstein's style of writing is to clarify misconceptions related to how language works. More specifically, he wants to draw the boundaries between an assertion's capacities and that which cannot be asserted, but which can only *be demonstrated* through such things as art, religion—and through Practice. Showing or proving something does not strictly imply an assertion or verbal description of what is being shown. Instead, it is something that is "intuited"—it is the absence of direct communication of significant insights. Examples and illustrations from everyday practice need to replace theories that aim to clarify, assert and uncover reality. The reason the concept of Showing is important is that it gives a description of silent/nothing in-practice and use, as language-is-use, an important empirical focus. It is essential to show a type of use which is not always suitable to assert, but rather is shown and described.

Third, there is "active nothing", a force of being potential which may evoke Dasein/nothing into innovations and a revolution of everyday life. Such a longing for radical innovation, history-making and revolution can take many guises: apocalyptic Heideggerianism (there are other Heideggerianisms), the neo-Nietzschean obliteration of "Man" or the utopianism that one finds in terrorism. This version of active nihilism is best expressed in Vaneigem's slogan "creativity plus a machine gun is an unstoppable combination" (Critcley 2007, p. 13). Even though there may be important issues such as a restoration of everyday life ("a cathedral of your own") and the rejection of homo faber (the reduction of human life to economy) in active nihilism, it seems like a theoretical and practical dead end.

The challenge is that if one rejects the first two responses to nothing by either (*a*) rejecting nothing as a pseudo-problem with a fallacious metaphysical philosophy or (*b*) failing to respond to the problem in passive acceptance, then the third response may appear too "revolutionary" or radical. The view of an (entrepreneurial) revolution of everyday life or the framework of "nothing" as a potential in revolutionary innovation may tell only half the story. Paradoxically, there is something too *reactive* in this sense about the very framing of active nothing—it may be too negatively obsessed with what it seeks to oppose and risks failing to comprehend the phenomenon of everyday life and being-in-the world in its challenge to overcome it. For example, in *Disclosing New Worlds*, Spinoza, Flores, and Dreyfus (1997) tend to advocate this view when they present illuminating examples of entrepreneurial history-making and radical innovations or "changes in the way in which we understand and deal with ourselves and things" (p. 2). They avoid subject-object fixation when they write about anomalies and disclosed worlds, and there seem to be some major innovation activities and skills embedded in their entrepreneurial analyses, which may be connected with central aspects and assumptions of Nothing (see more on this issue in chapter 3).

I would like to try to delineate a *fourth* response to nothing, one which I think borrows heavily from the second and third responses. With this fourth response, it is not only a question of overcoming nothing in a radical innovation, history-making and the skill of cultural innovation, because such an understanding could imprison us all the more firmly in the very logic I am trying to leave behind. Rather than overcoming nothing, in history-making it is a question of *sensitize* it, dwell in "nothing". That is to say, how entrepreneurs transform our background practices through history-making is not the pivotal question, but rather how entrepreneurs dwell in everyday life and (nothing) practices. Here, Nothing does not need extraordinary intentions or radical situations. It can arise in the most innocuous of situations: sitting on the train distractedly reading a book and overhearing conversations, one is suddenly seized by the feeling of meaninglessness, by the radical distinction between yourself and the world in which you find yourself.

The reason the concept of Showing is important is that it gives a description of silent/nothing in-practice and use, as language-is-use, an important empirical focus. It is essential to show a type of use which is not always suitable to assert, but rather is shown and described. However, it may be tempting to propose a main strategy, namely that Nothing should be made explicit through different mechanism for exchanging knowledge (by using metaphors, analogies, models, theories, etc.). It is important to be aware that not all Nothing can be made explicit (conceptualized) and externalized in this manner. There is no doubt that the "externalization" strategy is important, but it underestimates ways of showing the Nothing aspects within entrepreneurial practice. The nothing perspective states that all our aspects of nothing can potentially be shown in practice, but there will always be emerging and withdrawing new nothings and Being. Hence, the objectification of Being (Dasein) and Nothing is critical in the search for an objective understanding of Being itself facilitated by "being ahead of oneself" (Ricour 2006, p. 347). This is because humans are aware first and foremost of Being alive, and then we attempt to make sense of (entrepreneurial) life in thought and language (Heidegger 1962). However, it is possible to show how the entrepreneur retrospectively uses several aspects of Nothing. By conducting vignettes and examples, I illustrate some of the potential and possibilities in Nothing and Being (and certainly some of the limitations) in chapter 6. While I am reliant on some retrospective data, which may influence the completeness of examples and lead to "rationalized" versions of data, I think it is still possible to show how Nothing might play a role in entrepreneurial practice. Further, in chapter 7, a model of Nothing is presented along the lines of an "externalization" strategy, even though contemplating

Nothing does not mean showing a full-fledged picture of the vitality of the aspects of Nothing.

I do not think any of this (1, 2, 4) in principle cuts against more semantic and "epistemologized" approaches to Nothing because such views need not be conceived of to require a commitment to the priority of the fundamental ontological project (I think Heidegger would 100 percent agree). In fact, it can be conceived in the opposite direction. Start with what might be called an accepted pluralism of Nothing Noths to indicate the idea that there may be several knowledge relations resting on Nothing, a model designed to both capture and show the essence and complexity of Nothing in entrepreneurial practice. Maybe what has been bugging me here is not that Heidegger privileges addressing the fundamental ontological issue over traditional epistemology or epistemological versions of Nothing but what sort of language and showing is adequate to justify the phenomenon of Nothing. This is a question of not only understanding Being (self-understanding) but also understanding Being in many ways that make us entrepreneurial and human. It is probably a good idea to consider the degree to which one ought to be an epistemological sceptic with regard to (pre)determined Nothing possibilities (more on this in chapter 2).

On the basis of interwovenness and the relationship between Being and Nothing, it may be helpful to refer to four different aspects that, as a whole, can describe vitality and complexity and enable the articulation-potential of Nothing:

1. The functional aspect concerns the movement from Nothing to Being.
2. The phenomenal aspect concerns Being resting upon Nothing, but that Nothing can only be "communicated" indirectly via Being (Dasein).
3. The semantic aspect of the relationship between Being and Nothing refers to how meaning and knowledge can be created through the reciprocal movement from Nothing to Being and vice versa.
4. The (fundamental) ontological aspect is formed by the reflective structure that arises through Nothing.

The most fundamental of aspect 1 and 2 is that human life including entrepreneurship is known and experienced "before" language has the capacity to make sense of it, that is, having to make sense of it whilst in a prereflective awareness and what he called our average everydayness (Heidegger 1962). From the three aspects of Nothing that I have defined so far, the functional (1), the phenomenal (2), and the semantic (3), it is possible to deduce a fourth aspect, which tells us what Nothing is nothing of. Ontologically, the other three aspects of Nothing rest upon a fundamental reflective structure. This four-way division, or operating with four aspects of Nothing, may also explain some of the development that occurs in the book. There is talk about how it is possible to describe and show the meaning of Nothing. In other words, it is the articulation-potential that we see in various ways in chapters 4 and 5. Chapter 4, "Vignettes and Examples", rests on factors 1, 2 and 4 and tries to avoid the epistemological question and the epistemic language that the third factor necessarily implies.

1.4 Heidegger and Entrepreneurially Oriented Research Literature

Heidegger never (as far as I know) explicitly deals with entrepreneurship, entrepreneurial management or being entrepreneurial. There may be several reasons for the lack of explicit "entrepreneurial" statements in his writings. One obvious reason is to be found in the difference between ontic and ontological entities. The term *ontic* refers to human existence, of which entrepreneurship is a part, in contrast to "Being in itself" as an ontological phenomenon. Heidegger (1962) distinguishes between (*a*) the "ontic" level of the factual (for human existence, the term *existential* was introduced), which is subject to observation and the plane on which phenomenologist moves, and (*b*) the "ontological", which requires a phenomenological description of the deep structures that explain the ontic (here, he uses the term existenzial to describe the structure of existence). For Heidegger (1962), entrepreneurship is thus only one among many ways of being, without necessarily having the distinctive characteristics of Being itself.

However, he makes some remarks about ongoing activity (Betrieb), especially in the context of showing what he terms "technology" and in connection with the critique of the Cartesian tradition and science. The act of driving on, industry, activity, for example as undertaking, pursuit, management and business, may be considered a pre-phase (leaping alongside) before beginning to take possession of its own essence (Heidegger 1977). This is a departure point to explore the term "technology" and its potential relation to entrepreneurship and being entrepreneurial. It is a question of the kind of distinct world the entrepreneurial practice or entrepreneurial organization is setting up and understanding the very nature of technology. It is not easy to grasp the meaning of the nature of technology: "The essence of technology is by no means anything technological" (Heidegger 1977, p. 4). Entrepreneurs are often realistic about the opportunities and threats of developing, using and implementing technological devices and perhaps more optimistic in the running and competitive advantage of their entrepreneurial firm. Therefore, it is first and foremost not so much the risks related to the use of technology in terms of certain tools, instruments, processes, gadgets, devices and so forth. There is a more profound danger in the totality taken for granted that reveals everything (entrepreneurial) that entrepreneurs are compelled to develop and employ all of these tools (Which I call "the applicable paradigm") and instruments. Under the dominion of this technology/applicable paradigm, Nothing is allowed to appear as it is in itself. The readiness for use becomes the most important quality, and being available to serve some end is most valued. Perhaps a critique of the very nature of technology and the readiness for use is present at various times even from (entrepreneurial) economists: "Since capitalist enterprise, by its very achievements, tends to automatize progress, we conclude that it tends to make itself superfluous—to break to pieces under the pressure of its own success" (Schumpeter 1987, p. 134).

There seem to be few remarks from Heidegger about the potential pitfalls and flaws in modern economics as a science and technological (ready-to-hand) system, although Heidegger (1927, p. 413) remarks the following:

> [E]ven that which is ready-to-hand can be made a theme for scientific investigation and determination. . . . The context of equipment that is ready-to-hand in an everyday manner, its historical emergence and utilization, and its factical role in Dasein—all these are objects for the science of economics. The ready-to-hand can become the "Object" of science without having to lose its character as equipment. A modification of our understanding of Being does not seem to be necessarily constitutive for the genesis of the theoretical attitude "towards Things".

If we assume that the views of opportunity in entrepreneurship share some fundamental assumptions, namely that entrepreneurship is mainly investigated through the lenses of (technological) ready-to-hand concepts such as decision-making and market (see Miller 2007), then it is not surprising that everyday entrepreneurs are framed or pictured under the same labels. There are perhaps some critical insights into this framing in *What Are Poets For?*, in which Heidegger denounces marketization (2001, pp. 114–115):

In place of all the world-content of things that was formerly perceived and used to grant freely of itself, the object-character of technological dominion spreads itself over the earth ever more quickly, ruthlessly and completely. Not only does it establish all things as producible in the process of production; it also delivers the products of production by means of the market. In self-assertive production, the humanness of man and the thingness of things dissolve into the calculated market value of a market which not only spans the whole earth as a world market, but also, as the will to will, trades in the nature of Being and thus subjects all beings to the trade of a calculation that dominates most tenaciously in those areas where there is no need of numbers.

Such a structural, applicable and trade-off understanding of the market is present in entrepreneurial theory. For example, Kirzner (1973) introduced an alternative view of entrepreneurship in order to understand the nature of the market process and the dynamic character of market competition. Kirzner's framework is among other things based on a combination of Hayek's and Mises's ideas about the entrepreneur as the driving force of the economy and spontaneous coordination. Kirzner (1973) draws attention to the alert entrepreneur or the entrepreneur's alertness and how he or she is systematically "attracted to notice suboptimalities because they respond to the scent of pure profit which accompanies such suboptimalities" (p. 174). Kirzner (1973) states that all the entrepreneur "needs is to discover where buyers have been paying too much and where sellers have been receiving too little" (p. 41). Hence, opportunities are regarded as caused by the imperfect knowledge of market participants, and they can be seized by anyone discovering their existence before others have done so. It seems obvious that denotes different possibilities and potentials in marked "thinking" (possibilities in the marked as existence "discovery" and opportunity discovery serves different purposes, even though they do not need to be mutually exclusive).

Heidegger's potential for offering insights into entrepreneurial and innovation research has not received much attention despite the striking resemblance between the entrepreneurial and economic need for newness (Schumpeter 1987) and a reading of Heidegger's thinking as the philosophy of newness (Chattopadhyay and Srivastava 2007). Shionoya (2010); Spinoza, Flores, and Dreyfus (1997); Shaw, Tsai Dun-Hou, Ted, and Amjadi (2011) and Berglund (2007) are some of the few who have commented upon this issue. For example, Shionoya (2010, p. 191) observes the following:

> Schumpeter, from the Austrian school of economics, criticized the static nature of mainstream economics and took a unique approach to dynamic economics based on the concept of innovation and development. However, his economic theory is part of his concept of a universal social science: he had a much broader vision of society based on a typology of Dasein, though he did not use this ontological term.

Further, Shionoya (2010) points out Heidegger's term "leap" (*Sprung*) as a form of innovation, prefiguring the "turn" (*Kehre*) from his early to late work (p. 195). It is indicated that such a "turn" serves the same purpose as creative innovation did for Schumpeter as an *event* (p. 197). Heidegger's turn toward poetics also adds more dynamism to his old concepts, namely "the relationship between the conferring of Being by 'projection' and the emergence of the truth of Being from the state of *'thrownness'*" (p. 195). Shionoya (2010) concludes that this fusion of Schumpeter and Heidegger allows a reconciliation of these two concepts through "*Dasein as the thrown projector*" (p. 198). Perhaps Shionoya (2010) is right about Schumpeter's implicit Heideggerian thinking with regard to Dasein, even though it seems that there is more to gain by understanding how creative destruction (Schumpeter) and (Gestell) technology (Heidegger) as comparable pre-knowledge structures create new realities and existences.

However, it is possible to move from an implicit and speculative (Dasein) phenomenology to a more explicit phenomenological stance towards entrepreneurship. One version of this explicit phenomenological stance and approach is found in Spinoza, Flores, and Dreyfus's (1997) work *Disclosing New Worlds: Entrepreneurship, Democratic Action, and the Cultivation of Solidarity*. The authors focus on the skill of cultural innovation and provide insight into how in practice, entrepreneurs have a skill that enables them to identify and recognize the significance of anomalies:

> Our main goal is to show how entrepreneurial practices, the practices of virtuous citizens, and the practices of solidarity cultivation are ultimately grounded in and integrated by a crucial skill that human beings in the West have had for at least 2500 years.
>
> (Spinoza, Flores, and Dreyfus 1997, p. 2)

This is a bold and revolutionary theoretical perspective that introduces a new intellectual practice that works through examples to sensitize us to the subtle details and anomalies not immediately experienced in everyday practices. We are at our best, they say, when "we become sensitive to anomalies that enable us to change the style of our culture" (p. 181). Such a view could also be connected with a theory of "Nothing".

Even though entrepreneurs (and researchers) in a hermeneutical language are "always already" and on the way to becoming more than they already are, there is what we might call a *Nothing condition* to some of the changes we may observe in them. There is an unfolding such that their possible ends are already "there" in their beginnings. As a result, there is (or can be) a distinctive "Nothing" to our being, such that *from within*, not only but also can the earlier phases of those Nothings' activity be indicative to us (i.e. in style) of what is to come later. Entrepreneurs can then respond to their (Nothing) activities in an *anticipatory* way, projecting new possible worlds. Spinoza, Flores, and Dreyfus (1997) show the skills of grasping anomalies. Maybe the feeling of Nothing is sometimes involved, that is, entrepreneurs do not feel "at home" when anomaly is grasped.

When they propose the crucial "anomaly" skill, they also reject the notion that there could be a pre-fixed ideal way to proceed, that is, an entrepreneurial step-by-step manual for business success or a standardized procedure that can be provided to offer how to progress and advance. The "Heideggerian" nature or essence of entrepreneurship would reject that there is any such set of procedures. At this point, also Shaw, Tsai Dun-Hou, Ted, and Amjadi (2011) seem to be in line with Spinoza, Flores, and Dreyfus (1997) when they state the following:

> Phenomenological research cannot begin with the idea that we are going to improve, progress and advance, or fix things up. We must use a Heideggerian insight into the nature of truth to provide us with access to that which occurs as entrepreneurship.
>
> (p. 12)

Here, truth (*alētheia*) means the uncovering (and simultaneously covering) of beings (objects), and this perspective enables Heidegger to say that human beings including entrepreneurs exist "in the truth". The uncovering of beings including those beings that are the occurrent, that is, physical entities of entrepreneurship (Shaw, Tsai Dun-Hou, Ted, and Amjadi 2011). It may not be self-evident how this radical notion of truth could be studied or how a phenomenological (Heideggerian) perspective may "understand" entrepreneurial practice. Berglund (2007) presents a comprehensive overview of phenomenological methods in his study of entrepreneurship, and he does much to relate (potential) entrepreneurial research to the phenomenology of Heidegger. He emphasizes that if we wish to understand this in more detail, we need to know how the entrepreneurial world is interpreted. We may need to explore what entrepreneurship means to the people involved (Berglund 2007). In a similar vein, Åsvoll (2012, p. 71) says this:

> Taking this perspective, entrepreneurs cannot be studied outside the context in which they are regarded as entrepreneurs. Such research which aims at re-searching entrepreneurship can imply describing a transcendent (Da-sein) quality of entrepreneurship. Even though this quality cannot be defined a priori because it would destroy the very nature of becoming, entrepreneurs cannot be said to operate without context, i.e. without other people, without a network, without the basics such as a market or customers.

However, such contexts are not just characterized by deliberate, analytical and conscious entrepreneurial actions but rest upon a practical, intuitive and automatized practice and self-understanding. In ordinary everyday life, we tend to be locked into routine, and being preoccupied by practical tasks (Zuhanden) and busy with their execution, we rarely question the sense of the whole system of cares, goals and activities.

References

Åsvoll, H. (2012). On Heidegger, "theory of Nothing" and entrepreneurship: A prologue to an entrepreneurial philosophy of nothing. *Academy of Entrepreneurship Journal*, 18(1), 55–75.

Berglund, H. (2007). Opportunities as existing and created: A study of entrepreneurs in the Swedish mobile internet industry. *Journal of Enterprising Culture*, 15(3), 243–273.

Chattopadhyay, D. & Srivastava, B. N. (2007). The concept of newness. *Journal of Management Concepts and Philosophy*, 2(3), 240–245.

Critcley, S. (2007). *Very Little Almost Nothing: Death, Philosophy and Literature*. London: Routledge.

Heidegger, H. (1977). The question concerning technology. In W. Lovitt (ed.), *The Question Concerning Technology and Other Essays*. New York: Harper & Row Publishers.

Heidegger, H. (2001). What are poets for? In *Poetry, Language, Thought*. (Trans.) A. Hofstader. New York: Harper & Row Publishers.

Heidegger, M. (1927/1962). *Being and Time*. New York: Harper & Row Publishers.

Heidegger, M. (1976/1993). Was ist Metaphysik?. In *M. Heidegger, Wegmarken, Gesamtausgabe*. (Trans.) V. Klostermann, English translation as (Heidegger 1993). Frankfurt: Vittorio Klostermann.

Kirzner, I. (1973). *Competition and Entrepreneurship*. Chicago: University of Chicago Press.

Kirzner, I. (1997). Entrepreneurial discovery and the competitive market process: An Austrian approach. *Journal of Economic Literature*, 35, 60–85.

Miller, K. D. (2007). Risk and rationality in entrepreneurial processes. *Strategic Entrepreneurship Journal*, 1(1–2), 57–74.

Ricour, P. (2006). *Memory, History and Forgetting*. (Trans.) K. McLoughlin & D. Pellaur. London: The University of Chicago Press.

Sarasvathy, S. D., Dew, N., Velamuri, S. R. & Venkataraman, S. (2003). Three views of entrepreneurial opportunity. In Z. J. Acs & D. B. Audretsch (eds.), *Handbook of Entrepreneurship Research: An Interdisciplinary Survey and Introduction*. Dordrecht, The Netherlands: Kluwer, 141–160.

Schumpeter, J. A. (1987). *Capitalism, Socialism and Democracy*, 6th ed. Counterpoint ed. London: Unwin Paperbacks.

Shaw, R. K., Tsai Dun-Hou, S., Ted, L. Y. C. & Amjadi, M. (2011). *The ontology of entrepreneurship: A Heideggerian perspective*. Proceedings of Australia and New Zealand Academy of Management. Available at SSRN: https://ssrn.com/abstract=1976735

Shepherd, D. A. (2017). Decision making in entrepreneurship: Introduction. In *Decision Making in Entrepreneurship: Selected Papers of Dean A. Shepherd*. xi–xiv. DOI: 10.4337/9781784716042.

Shionoya, Y. (2010). Hermeneutics and the Heidegger = Schumpeter thesis. *The American Journal of Economics and Sociology*, 69(1), 188–202.

Simon, H. A. (1979). Rational decision making in business organizations. *American Economic Review*, 69(4), 493–513.

Spinoza, C., Flores, F. & Dreyfus, H. (1997). *Disclosing New Worlds: Democratic Action and the Cultivation of Solidarity*. Cambridge: MIT Press.

Wittgenstein, L. (2005). *Tractacus Logico Philosophicus*. London: Routledge.

Part 1

Some Central Assumptions of Entrepreneurial Theory and the Potential of Nothing Entrepreneurial Theory

The aim of this part is to contrast basic assumptions of entrepreneurial theory with the demands for a theory of nothing. Entrepreneurial theory is by no means an expression of a wholly unified, one-voiced and monologic scientific practice. Several developments in the field have made entrepreneurial theory more dynamic, context- and process-oriented. However, some of the basic assumptions in traditional and relatively new entrepreneurial theory remain (Alvarez 2005). As Gartner (2001) suggests, in the field of entrepreneurship we are too often unaware of the assumptions that we make in our theoretical perspectives, and an unwillingness to entertain alternative assumptions has without doubt hampered the development of theory in the field of entrepreneurship. This chapter will show why certain assumptions make it harder to acknowledge and describe the potential of the Nothing entrepreneurial theory, and consequently we may become more critically aware of our assumptions. More specifically, three assumptions that underlie entrepreneurial theory are proposed and compared to basic features of Nothing. We examine in turn three pairs of assumptions: becoming versus being, decision-making versus dwelling and active versus passive.

2 Why Assumptions in Entrepreneurial Theory Do Not Work in Explaining Phenomena of Nothing

To shed light on the basic features of nothing, it is necessary to take a closer look at three assumptions constituting entrepreneurial theory, that is to say, becoming, decision-making and active or activity. By contrasting these assumptions with Nothing "assumptions" such as Being, being-in-the-world/dwelling and passive/passivity, it is possible to lay the groundwork and to realize what may be gained by a theory of Nothing perspective in entrepreneurial research, theory and education (see chapter 6).

2.1 Becoming Versus Being

Here, the emphasis on becoming and consequently the underplaying of Being is exemplified by two dominant research perspectives in entrepreneurial theory: first various forms of opportunity views and second the narrative or prosaic stream of research.

How the entrepreneur manages and relates to opportunities is currently regarded as a key term for understanding entrepreneurship and economic change (Fiet 1996; Gartner 2001; Shane and Venkataram 2000; Sarasvathy et al. 2003; Eckhardt and Shane 2003; Short, Ketchen, Shook, and Ireland 2010). For example, Venkataraman (1997) and Shane and Venkataraman (2000) argue that the relation between the entrepreneur and opportunity should be the distinctive domain of entrepreneurship research. There are several approaches to research in "entrepreneurial opportunity" (Shepherd 2011), and we may identify three different and contrasting views or processes, with different labels, such as allocative-, discovery- and creative-processes (Buchanan and Vanberg 1991); opportunity recognition, opportunity discovery and opportunity creation (Sarasvathy et al. 2003). Those views on opportunity explicitly advocate distinct positions on the issue, such as the ontological status of opportunities.

In their treatise title "The Language of Opportunity", Gartner, Carter, and Hills (2003) pose fundamental questions with respect to how entrepreneurial opportunities have been studied from two contrasting ontological positions. The first is the positivist/realist position predominant among North American researchers, which suggests that opportunities exist independently in the environment, waiting to be discovered or recognized. The second is an alternate interpretive or social constructionist position, more prevalent in the European research tradition, which suggests that entrepreneurial opportunities emerge, i.e. are created, on the basis of the entrepreneur's interpretation of environmental forces. It is also claimed that entrepreneurial opportunity is best understood not as a static object that posed statically somewhere on the epistemological continuum between the subjective and objective but as the initial starting condition of a process vector that begins somewhere on that continuum but always moves across it into increasing epistemological objectivity. Then, epistemologically, opportunity is the creative process of embedding a venture ever more deeply into the objective institutions where it needs to exist to thrive (Mcbride, Wuebker, and Grant 2003).

Such underlying assumptions and insights of "opportunity thinking" are also transferred to entrepreneurial practice. Dutta and Crossan (2005), for example suggest that their research has several useful insights for practitioners:

> first it suggests that entrepreneurial opportunities may be usefully analysed on the basis of either of the two contrasting ontological positions positivist/ realist provided that we adopt a learning perspective. . . . [T]his we believe, provides entrepreneurs with a very useful process view of opportunities. . . . [W]e suggest that once entrepreneurs adopt this expanded process view of opportunities that cross multiple levels of analysis, they stand to benefit immensely.
>
> (p. 444)

Despite the strive of nailing opportunity (theories) and entrepreneurship practice, it has been pointed out that entrepreneurship research lacks a coherent theoretical consensus or framework that "explains the emergence and development of entrepreneurial opportunities" (Companys and McMullen 2007, p. 302). Shane (2003) has suggested a reasonable thesis on the possible sources of opportunities prior to emergence (for example, when he discusses the environmental context for productive entrepreneurship). Yet scholarly understanding still appears to be limited particularly with respect to the development of these opportunities in practice, that is to say most studies take opportunities for granted (ibid.). Although research in these opportunity traditions has produced a significant body of knowledge explaining how entrepreneurs engage with opportunities (both ontological and epistemological), the phenomenon is believed to be self-evident and taken for granted. The assumption that opportunity strongly relates to the entrepreneurial world implies a correspondence theory of truth.

A correspondence theory of truth, in the strict sense, denotes the conformity of thought (opportunity) with its object (entrepreneurial world). The basic idea was named correspondence by early analytic language philosophers (Bertrand Russell, the early Wittgenstein, Rudolf Carnap and Moritz Schlick), who advocated a picture theory of language. Their purpose was to find propositions (statements) that would be the "logical atoms" of verifiable knowledge of the world. In more simple terms, truth consists in correspondence between a claim about the world and the world. For a statement to be true, the world must be the way that the statement says it is. It must correspond to the facts. Thus, a claim about a theoretical entity is true only in the event the theoretical entity is as it is claimed to be. For example, the sentence "opportunities are the starting point of entrepreneurial practice" is true if and only if opportunities are the starting point of entrepreneurial practice.

Heidegger dubs correspondence theories of truth the "traditional" and "usual" concepts of truth and he considers their exposition in ancient and scholastic philosophy (Heidegger 1962, p. 257). Heidegger finds such positivist accounts of truth meaningful, and apparently, it is very effective and applicable in entrepreneurial research. The generic word Heidegger prefers to refer to this form of truth is the Latin *adaequatio*, because it indicates "similarity" which implies a human judgement that involves an equation whilst remaining silent on the content of the judgement. This seems to be the leading account of truth that appears in entrepreneurship research dominated by opportunity and decision-making. This may seem like a waterproof approach until truth is considered otherwise. However, in a secondary sense, truth is correspondence, because our practices have opened up the Being of beings for us in the first place. For example the practice of working and observing cloud-chambers lets electrons show up for us, or become present in "the clearing"; or as teachers come into their own as teachers by learning to recognize, cultivate and then help develop their students' skills. Or as the entrepreneur comes into her own by observing marked activities and perhaps allows opportunities to appear to her. Only after these disclosive events have occurred can one gauge the match between "the facts" about electrons, teachers, entrepreneurs and our judgements about them. Our practices reveal or disclose the being of beings to us, yet every disclosure of being (given that it is always finitely mediated by practice) is also a concealment and an untruth. Every truth also harbours untruth, a concealing, which means that every vocabulary we devise which lets the being of beings be manifested to us can never exhaust the being of beings, can never be a complete, definitive and final vocabulary, and thus in some measure lets distortion and less rigour slip through.

It is possible to argue that positivist modes of enquiry, functionalistic assumptions (correspondence theory of truth) in entrepreneurship have resulted in the researcher viewing the "entrepreneur's world as something that can be judged from outside using 'hard' concepts" (i.e. Perren and Ram 2004, p. 91). However, such subject/subjectivity-object/objectivity entrepreneurial thinking and distinctions between Being and beings somehow wind up construing Being as a being, as a determinate, determinable and that this makes a genuine understanding of Being as that which lets beings "appear" or "come into the clearing" for entrepreneurial practice research very difficult. It seems like entrepreneurial theorizing about the ontological status of opportunities proceeds on the mistaken assumption that Being can be fully grasped by means of an all-encompassing and universal opportunity theory; whether or not it is more realist, constructivist or pragmatist accounts (a "general theory of Being" in a Heideggerian sense), we lose a sense of the presence of Being in our (entrepreneurial) lives.

As such, opportunity in theory (either ontological subjective or objective) does not seem to have anything to do with Nothing, i.e. how (potential) opportunities sometimes reveal themselves first as (existential) possibilities, perhaps at a glance, before being sustained, epistemologized and a part of decision-making practice in entrepreneurial management. Here, the original entrepreneurial Being and Nothing is-duplicated and ends up in a "closed-being". Such a being-duplicate contributes to the being-in-becoming view, where a "closed being" plays a role inasmuch as it moves becoming (epistemologized) opportunities. It is also possible to find another version of this very dominant (closed) being-in-becoming view in entrepreneurial theory, more specifically anchored in what might be called a prosaic and narrative perspective.

On Prosaic Research and Becoming

One research trend has largely contributed to substantiate the importance of dialogue in becoming and in entrepreneurial processes, as well as in entrepreneurship. The narrative and prosaic perspectives, among other things, have been in opposition to a one-sided focus on the individual, and important dimensions of this research have been a subsequent undervaluation of relational learning resources, and an upvaluation of everyday life. For instance, one statement proposes that

> *By approaching entrepreneurship as a prosaics, we can situate its formation there where it happens and where it can happen: as lived*

experience, as story, as drama, as conversation, as performance, in all its everydayness.

(Steyaert 2003, p. 19)

In a convincing fashion, this perspective has become the subject of research closely related to practice and oriented towards processes, with Bakhtin as a central theoretical source. Within an epistemological framework, the point of departure is empirical and conceptual research from numerous researchers. Leading figures of this kind of research (Steyaert 1995, 1997, 1998, 2003; Hjorth and Steyaert 2004; Steyaert and Hjorth 2003) have been important contributors to (epistemological) entrepreneurial research since the mid-1990s. Many other researchers have employed different approaches to promote the significance of entrepreneurial narrative and discursive and dialogic research (i.e. Mantere, Aula, Schildt, and Vaara 2013; Ahl 2002; Boutaiba 2004; Cosgel 1996; Fleming 2001; Johansson 2004; Hjorth and Johannisson 2009).

A description may prove essential for understanding epistemological interpretation. Such an ontological interpretation is further reinforced by statements such as:

In stressing "mess", one acknowledges a becoming-ontology. . . . This mess is called by Deleuze (1995, p. 138) "holes", the parts of our life where our identity crashes, our voice stutters: "That's what I find interesting in people's lives, the holes, the gaps, sometimes dramatic, but sometimes not dramatic at all. There are catalepsies, or a kind of sleep-walking through a number of years, in most lives. Maybe it's in these holes that movement takes place". Calling things a "mess" should not be seen as something unpleasant or negative, but as part of the open and creative becoming of life, inexhaustible and unfinalizable.

(Steyaert 2004, p. 11)

. . . conclude that the identity construction in this chapter deals with an ontological aspect—a theory of being (Somers 1994). I find that an analysis of identity construction and life course contributes to the entrepreneurship field in that a narrative contributes to the understanding of becoming an entrepreneur.

(Foss 2003, p. 102)

From an ontology of becoming, in which processes can be described and understood, it becomes clear that entrepreneurial processes of creation emerge.

(Hjorth and Johannisson 2009, p. 64)

Here ontology is presented as a type of becoming of life (entrepreneur). Nevertheless, the central point is that the dialogue's existential or ontological aspect is often emphasized rather than empirical analyses, and as such, it may seem as if ontological dialogue is intentionally given a leading role in the epistemological approach of Hjorth and Steyaert (2004); Steyaert and Hjorth (2003) and Foss (2003), amongst others. A further indication of this is found in Steyaert's (2004) focus on the radical significance of social or relational constructionism, which implies:

> de-centring particular individuals (that is, entrepreneurs) and, instead, centring relational processes; letting go of talk about individuals, mind operations (including sense making) and knowledge, to instead talk of relational processes as inter-actions that (re)construct identities and worlds as local rationalities or cultures.
>
> (p. 257)

A reasonable interpretation is that an entrepreneurial understanding of relational constructionism may be viewed as an expression of Bakhtin's ontological project, where the objective also lies on a general level; "relational constructionism is best viewed as a thought style, as a 'theory of theories'" (Steyaert 2004, p. 258).

Fletcher and Watson (2006, pp. 12–13) indicate that the empirical subjects may be characterized in a certain way;

> Relational analysis takes account of the human individual, but sees the individual as a social self that is always in interaction with others and has a continually emergent identity. It pays attention to the inter-subjective aspects of exchange but, at the same time, it highlights the communal tradition and history of relationships and meanings in which we are all located. Incorporating Bakhtin's (1981) theory of dialogism and scepticism about the capacity of a single authority to monopolize meaning (Gergen 1999, p. 122), dialogic, emergent and relational thinking replaces the traditional and dominant notion of the entrepreneurial "self" with a view of entrepreneurial identities as expressions of relationship.

Here one may get the impression that the words and the utterances are "dialogized" from a social self and the entrepreneurs' mutual involvement. This means that the utterances or words may open up for a new understanding, all the while allowing the presence of a large degree of "intersubjectivity". By promoting the application of terms such as dialogue, intersubjectivity and identity in an empirical analysis of entrepreneuring and learning, a certain "epistemological" interpretational approach is taken. This is shown in that intersubjectivity presumes that the subject or individual exists (fully) before entering a knowledge-producing intersubjectivity.

Viewed in the context of Being, the bearer or a representative for others outside of itself, it will not do to view a subject or entrepreneur in this way, according to a Heideggerian interpretation of Being. Being does not as such stand in any relation to the subject (or object) status of the entrepreneur, but rather postulates a kind of possible intangible idea of moving beyond subject–object relations, a Being in or *trans-being* (primordial condition) which is not the same as the "expressions of relationship" and intersubjectivity. In other words, Being exists in a fundamental way prior to the entrepreneur, understood as an individual. This means that Being as a subject/individual does not define the Being; rather it is the Being that constitutes the entrepreneur. Even though Being might be preserved in such entrepreneurial theorizing, to have a sensation of Being and Being entrepreneurial may have other contours to it than the knowledge-developing processes. As such, it seems reasonable to say that Being has its role as Being-in-becoming and not as becoming-in-Being. Related to this status of Being and becoming is the distinction between decision-making and dwelling.

2.2 Decision-Making Versus Dwelling

Many researchers in entrepreneurship have used the term "entrepreneurial decision-making" to label their theories and empirical findings, for example Busenitz and Barney (1997), Lévesque and MacCrimmon (1997); Forlani and Mullins (2000); Sarasvathy (2001); Simon and Houghton (2002); Mullins and Forlani (2005); Lévesque and Schade (2005) and Gustafsson (2006). Some academics suggest that decision-making is the most fundamental type of behaviour exhibited by individuals in organizations (March and Simon 1966; Cooke and Slack 1984), which may also include entrepreneurial management. Schade and Burmeister-Lamp (2009) conclude that entrepreneurial decision-making bears the potential of a scientific paradigm, and addresses the need to stimulate theory development to establish such a paradigm. The traditional view of entrepreneurship and management maintains that entrepreneurship is a rational set of activities that considers entrepreneurs performing functions such as planning, control, organizing and leading (Mukhi, Hampton, and Barnwell 1988); i.e. executing decisions along many functions. Examples of decisions by entrepreneurs explored from different research streams are whether or not to exploit an opportunity? how to enter a market? (Camerer and Lovallo 1999); how to manage effectuation? (Sarasvathy 2001); how to raise capital? (Timmons, Spinelli, and Zacharakis 2005); how to deal with competitors, network and alliances?

(Bass 1969); how to manage rapid growth? (Churchill and Lewis 1983). These examples framed as questions indicate the presence of an entrepreneurial decision-making paradigm. In the following, I will not attempt to provide accurate answers to these questions, but rather to describe some less-recognized aspects of entrepreneurial decision-making as it unfolds in the (becoming) entrepreneurial practice.

For example, much of the academic status and legitimacy of business schools or institutes of entrepreneurship derives from the way they seem to signify applied "decision-making knowledge", as well as the capacity to conduct decision-making aimed at eventually creating new ventures. This "applied" or tool-based view in isolation may reduce decision-making to the (mechanical) application of preconceived rules for optimalization. It may trivialize decision-making, and makes it harder to show the entrepreneurs in pre-decision moments of a particular and unpredictable kind.

The aim is to show that the tendency to portray decision-making in terms of intention (opportunity-exploitation), purposefulness, goal-orientation (market behaviour) and action (effectuation) overlooks and underplays dwelling, immanence and immanent "decisions". In challenging this dominant decision-making view, it is possible to argue that decisions and decision-making takes place in a more fundamental *dwelling* mode, in which entrepreneurs' identities/being and their decisions are simultaneously and immediate through direct engagement with the world they inhabit. In other words, practical actions and dwelling mode precede individual entrepreneurial identity and decision intent.

But "What *is* dwelling?" Heidegger (1978) raises the question at the beginning of *Building Dwelling Thinking*. There are many interpretations of the term dwelling, and I will not go into detail. In a sense, "to dwell is to live a life that is informed by a particular experience—the experience or feeling of being 'at home' in one's world. To dwell is to live a life that is informed by the experience of the place in which one lives as a dwelling-place, a homeland" (Young 2000, p. 194).

It is possible to say that dwelling is a sort of non-purposeful existence in time. The concept of dwelling can be described as a mode of *at-home* existence where a being who is active (or perhaps passive, see 4.3) within the world is totally immersed within its environment. This immersion of the entrepreneur, student and researcher in a specific context establishes a conditional mode of engagement called dwelling that precedes mental representation and deliberate purposeful action, or *building* as Heidegger (1978) calls it. For example, the entrepreneur dwells in that she receives the marked as marked, she awaits profit as profit (or other values such as social issues), she initiates her own nature and capacity as nature.

There is much more to be said on dwelling, but for our purposes, it is important merely to underscore that there is an emphasis on the primarily practical way in which we grasp or understand beings, including beings such as ourselves. Things are presented to us as beings to be used in our personal and everyday practice; any one item-for-use derives its usefulness from being one node in a network of tools, procedures, traditions and skills. This "referential totality" constitutes our specific dwelling places, "passivity" and approach to reality. It is important to note that at the bottom of these dwelling places and practices lies not a theory, but Nothing and being, which cannot be fully captured in any theory (a significant point of contact with the later Wittgenstein). One approach to trying to understand the interwoven fix (my interpretation) between "referential totality", and in particular dwelling and Nothing, would be to begin by focusing on Heidegger's presentation of the apparently opposite or absence of dwelling, that is to say homelessness and Nothing. The early Heidegger (1962) concludes that dwelling is impossible in the face of the "abyss (*Abgrund*)". To paraphrase Heidegger (1962), in the "absence (*Ab*) of the "ground (*grund*) which grounds", we cannot dwell. However, to use the language of the middle Heidegger, homelessness (which stems from Nothing) is the *Grundstimmung*, the "fundamental mood" of Dasein's "being-in-the-world" and it is the fundamental mood of *Being and Time* itself (Young 2000). Most importantly, it is possible to speak of a reappraisal of the aspect of nothing and homelessness (*unheimlichkeit*), that is to say, there is an intimate connection between dwelling and nothing. A related "connection" or "intertwined" assumption is that of activity and passivity, even though at first it is an analytical advantage to present them as opposites or mutually exclusive.

2.3 Activity Versus Passivity

In order to describe what I would call the activity assumption in entrepreneurial theory some aspects of activity in theory (venture opportunity creation and cognition) need to be explored. In some way, it seems as if the assurances that we give to entrepreneurship come from structures or forms of activity or something activity-like. Mindful that "activity driven" theories do not discuss in depth the importance of passivity, at long last it seems useful to show how passivity might work.

But first, what is entrepreneurship activity? Entrepreneurship is apparently about the pursuit of opportunities, and decision-making (in entrepreneurial theory). Entrepreneurship theory attempts to explain entrepreneurial activity dominated by notions of process, method, design, decision-making, opportunity, action. It is hard to imagine entrepreneurial research and theory at all without those terms that denote certain activities. For example, entrepreneurship is described by Shane (2003) as an activity that "involves the discovery, evaluation and exploitation of opportunities to introduce new goods and services, ways of organising, market processes and raw materials through organising efforts that had previously not existed" (p. 4). Discovering opportunities is considered the essential, critical first step in the entrepreneurial process, one from which exploitation and entrepreneurial profit will follow.

In short, this definition of entrepreneurship—"the identification, evaluation, and exploitation of opportunities"—is distinctive and seems to serve as a paradigmatic foundation. This definition has become the most cited and applied definition in the field (Aldrich and Cliff 2003). However, can we really expect entrepreneurship to be fixated on opportunities? Is entrepreneurship really so predictable? As previously addressed (2.1), researchers have traditionally accepted an opportunity perspective; a view dominated by a linear, staged-activity approach to new venture creation; that is, to identify an opportunity, develop the concept, determine resource requirements, acquire resources, develop a business plan, implement the plan, manage the venture and exit (Morris 1998). A statement made by Van de Ven, Angle, and Poole (2000) is indicative: "An appreciation of the temporal sequence of activities in developing and implementing new ideas is fundamental to the management of entrepreneurship, because entrepreneurs need to know more than the input factors required to achieve desired outcomes. They are centrally responsible for directing the innovating process with the proverbial 'black box' between inputs and outcomes. To do this, the entrepreneur needs a 'road map' indicating how and why the innovating journey unfolds, and the paths that are likely to lead to success or failure" (p. xviii).

Even though such staged-venture creation activities may be viewed as more dynamic and process-oriented, there is still unexplored activity in "the proverbial black box". Here, the claim is that the ontologies involved in entrepreneurial (opportunity) activity are passing over the world, quickly jumping to specifics (stages, plans, sequences, resources etc.) and subjects that already imply a conception of being as *present*. In whatever pursuit an entrepreneurial researcher engages, her understanding of *that which is* in its *which-is-ness* is what is decisive for whatever is to be claimed. Ontology, that is, the primary stance we take on the meaning of Being, projects itself in its impressive decisiveness in further researching.

Another obvious example of *that-which-is understanding* is penetrating entrepreneurial cognition research. Cognition researchers are uncovering patterns in how entrepreneurs think and begin hypothesizing that specific ways of thinking are sources of competitive advantage and individual differentiation (Mitchell et al. 2002). Furthermore, entrepreneurial cognition is defined as "the knowledge structures that people use to make assessments, judgments, or decisions involving opportunity evaluation, venture creation, and growth" (Mitchell et al. 2002, p. 97). In other words, the question is no longer whether an individual can be an entrepreneur, but instead how an individual may benefit from "knowledge structures" and become entrepreneurial, create opportunities and act on them.

The work of Sarasvathy (2001, 2003), introduced the field to a new cognitive theory called effectuation. Sarasvathy's dissertation research incorporated think aloud, verbal protocols with forty-five expert entrepreneurs. The experimental methodology required subjects to "think aloud" as they made decisions and solved a set of ten typical problems that occur in a start-up. A theory of creative effectuation emerged from the data in contrast to its inverse, causation (linear process with emphasis on prediction, stability in context). Sarasvathy (2008) empirically discovered that effectual entrepreneurs see the world as open to a host of different possibilities; they fabricate as well as recognize new opportunities, make rather than find markets, accept and leverage failure and interact with a variety of stakeholders, all for the purpose of creating the future rather than trying to predict the future. Effectual principles (experimentation, affordable loss, flexibility and pre-commitments) as well as effectuation itself were revealed as being positively related to new venture performance (Cai, Guo, and Liu 2017; Read, Song, and Smit 2009; Smolka, Verheul, and Burmeister-Lamp 2015). A lot of promising research is done and a stream of research is established. In short, the overall research question is to understand how successfully entrepreneurs follow the same logic or mindset (i.e. effectual principles); in other words, the entrepreneurial mindset and disclosing dominant cognitive activity became all important. Therefore, framed in the background of entrepreneurial mindset and cognition, effectuation is a logic of distinctive and successful patterns of thinking. It seems like the cognitive effectual logic precedes behaviour, opportunities (they must be created by cognitive thinking) and even (existential) possibilities. When the cognitive activity always seems to come first, the entrepreneur may be depositioned through cognitive structures and, delineated with a discernible and dominating effectual logic, can foreclose on the very undecidedness by which the Nothing as conditions of entrepreneurial practice are made possible. Effectual logic can elucidate deeper structure from the experience of everyday entrepreneurial life, but this Nothing (passivity) of everyday life is beyond such structuring. A turn to Nothing (unstructured) and a consequent questioning of the purposeful confinement of entrepreneurial cognition and experience are, then, potentially significant, as we ask with what epistemological framing we might appreciate entrepreneurial being activity, and, in addition, whether this activity exhausts the experience of Being/Nothing/passivity-in-entrepreneurship?

More on Passivity

Passivity is not valued nor considered much in entrepreneurship. A phenomenological description of entrepreneurial (nothing) practice may show that this is a mistake. However, when we initially explore being entrepreneurial, the same inhibitions emerge that determine our relation to passivity in general. Just as it is a negative characteristic to describe somebody as "passive", there is also an impression that a more active engagement is conducive to entrepreneurship or being entrepreneurial. Paradigmatic perspectives such as (active) constructivism, constructionism, pragmatism and more theoretical terms such as decision-making, process, becoming, action framing the engaged and active entrepreneur indicates this conviction. Passivity in entrepreneurship is usually associated with failure and more precisely, treated as some form of entrepreneurial "black box" or non-entrepreneurial practice. By contrast, research on creation and process entrepreneurship tends to focus on the entrepreneur as "subject" rather than treated "object", where "subject" is often interpreted in terms of autonomy and activity.

The existential phenomenology of Nothing presented here places an emphasis on passivity and thus counters the current research emphasis on activity in entrepreneurship. This is not to deny but merely to supplement the significance of "active entrepreneurship". A few preparatory clarifications are in place. Firstly, a general reminder concerning the position taken here: it is not my purpose to argue against "active entrepreneurship". Secondly, the purpose in highlighting the significance of passivity is not to indicate that "doing nothing" would be the best attitude to embrace in entrepreneurship. Rather, passivity is an essential component of the experience, and it is helpful to consider how to deal with passivity. Importantly, passivity is nothing, but it does mean doing nothing. Passivity is not meant to signify that nothing occurs. It may be externally passive, but internally active. Passivity is complex and multi-faceted, and responding to an experience of passivity may be challenging, While passivity describes a general attitude of "letting-be" and applies to entrepreneurship as a whole, there is a more concrete part of entrepreneurship that may require passivity, but can also be prepared for more concretely by insights from phenomenology.

In order to describe the passivity it is necessary to know more about a certain kind of phenomenology. The terms "phenomenology" and "phenomenological" are frequently used in a broad sense to describe and represent perspectives for how we (the entrepreneur and researcher) immediately experience and perceive the world. In the following, I aim to acquire a more concrete understanding of what a specifically phenomenological approach may entail for an entrepreneurial practice. The starting point can be articulated in the form of the "Nothing" aspect: the latter can be understood as the start of a phenomenology that seeks to maintain the notion of being/Nothing in a pre-reflective and unpredictable practice that is again the very basis for the way (hermeneutical) interpretations occur.

Within a phenomenology concerned with the issue of a pre-reflective being/existence, it is important to be aware of the fact that "phenomenology" cannot be characterized through questions about *what* the content of the object is (*das sachhaltige Was*), but rather the why of research or of entrepreneurship (Heidegger 1962, p. 27). By the expression *"zu den Sachen selbst"* (Heidegger 1962, p. 27), the researcher and the entrepreneur are permitted to express their (research) process as it develops. On this backdrop, an important question can be intimated concerning *how* the entrepreneur's practice is understood in conjunction with the researcher's practice. The researcher and entrepreneur's self-understanding thus becomes a question of how, or as Heidegger (1960) puts it, a genuine methodical reflection:

> *Echte methodische Besinnung—die von leeren Erörterungen der Technik wohl zu unterscheiden ist—gibt deshalb zugleich Aufschluss über die Seinart des thematischen Seienden.*
>
> (p. 302)

The "method" in question is a matter of tracking down specific contexts that situate the researcher/entrepreneur or that make her who she is—that constitute the researcher's/entrepreneur's self-understanding. The tracking relies on an implicit meaning/understanding in a practice that creates hermeneutic situations and the (ontic) limitations and opportunities that are concealed therein. Self-understanding's situatedness opens for envisioning the researcher's research and the entrepreneur's practice as depending on how he understands himself. This type of ontological self-understanding cannot be reduced to actions and everyday decisions, nor can it be reduced to the concrete possibilities that derive from such choices. What is (includes Nothing) and what "defines" the researcher's and entrepreneur's daily practice/potential interpretations is always already based on one's fundamental orientation in the world. It may be interesting to try to articulate such a fundamental orientation/passivity or a life-project of which both research and entrepreneurial practice can be a part (more on this in chapter 6.2).

Like Heidegger, Gadamer (2004) also claims that phenomenology's quest for *"die Sache selbst"* must depend on an understanding in the world or a situation-conditioned determination of understanding. In this respect, it is possible to accept that a hermeneutic can value a phenomenological conception but also, to my mind, is "controlled" by Nothing. In the following, I present hermeneutical terms borrowed from Gadamer's perspective. The point of departure is that the researcher's interpretations must be based on understanding what already understands us or, in other words, that the truth precedes (the Cartesian) method. This means that Gadamer (2004) wishes to remove the belief in any certain researcher's premise outside or beyond a text/tradition that an objective interpreter maintains he/she is in possession of.

In the most radical sense, this is a matter of a preparedness that allows questions to be posed (and I will add allows Nothing), a worthiness to question, with one's own and others' prejudices. To ask the right questions is crucial for entry into relevant channels leading to understanding. One of the most central conditions for opportunity is to be seized by relevant channels, denoted by Gadamer (2004) as tradition (*Überlieferung*). Tradition can always overplay the text as the object of our understanding, and it has us in the palm of its hand at the very moment we make an attempt to understand. The act of understanding is in and of itself "controlled" by a "stimulation" that is not an act of subjectivity, but that derives from tradition. In other words, it is impossible to stand outside this kind of ontological, structural condition. Opportunity lies instead in "surrendering" oneself to tradition and Nothing and then allowing it to engender potential ways of understanding. Gadamer (2004) places emphasis on this when he writes, "Wir stehen vielmehr ständig in Überlieferung, und dieses Darinstehen ist kein vergegenständichendes Verhalten . . . eine grundlegende Voraussetzung, nämlich, sich von der Überlieferung *angesprochen* zu sehen" (pp. 286–287). To allow tradition and Nothing speak to us is the sole method by which to claim relevance and truth—a truth that, in research as well, goes beyond strategic choices and circular movements of understanding.

Summary and Reflection

Nothing negates the presupposition of Being as *present*. Instead, it is possible to point to Being as a *bringing forth into unconcealment*, a recovering or researching the most initial meaning of *presencing*. World as a *bringing forth* thus relies on the difference it makes, for an entrepreneur (researcher) in its individuality, i.e. that there is something instead of nothing. As such, the meaning of Being, and therefore of entrepreneurs (researchers) themselves, may escape actuality by contextualizing itself against a horizon of umbrella terms such as activity, becoming (dialogue, opportunity), decision-making and activity (cognition). If we characterize entrepreneurial theory and research captured or adopted in a becoming decision-making-activity picture, which I think is a rather uncontroversial premise, then there is not surprisingly less space for ontological-existence-Being related issues.

To apply an expression borrowed from Heidegger: "the more consciousness, the less being", indicating that the more becoming, the less Being.

Here, becoming may be considered a concept within (analytic) epistemology that denotes a distinction between consciousness and body or subject and object. On the contrary, being as a term in ontology denotes a coincidence of consciousness and the body or subject (self) and object (other) (Macann 2007). So, different formal principles (distinction and coincidence) could say something about different modes of awareness and experiences. For Heidegger this implies that the development of consciousness is paid for at the cost of a diminishment of the being-relation. Or as Macann (2007) says: "The more the human being develops itself, its conscious resources, the less it remains one with itself and with that in which it finds itself"(p. 20). This is apparently a controversial statement (although it may depend on how it is interpreted) that has radical implications both for entrepreneurial education/practice and entrepreneurial theorizing (see more in chapter 6.1, 6.2 and 6.3). Perhaps to question prevailing assumptions about activity and introducing passivity may show how conscious resources underplay Being/Nothing-in-the-world.

In the stratification and split into "passive and active" assumptions, the realm of passivity describes those acts that occur within being-in-the-world without the entrepreneur/researcher having to act on them, that is, without an obligation of consciously taking them up. This is in contrast to the realm of decision-making activity, in which the entrepreneurial subject knowingly directs its egoic regard to a particular object or purposively intends a particular act. One central feature of passivity necessarily entails that the entrepreneurial subject is not alone and monadic, but is always influenced by a world that is not only constituted but also constituting. This is to say that the world is not only constituted by the subject, but also helps to constitute that subject. As subjects, we not only act upon the world, but are acted upon by that world. In other words, the entrepreneur-in-the-world ventriqulates the in-between. This means that the very power of the subject, the subject's ability to constitute the world, is not something that the subject does on its own merit or because of its own inherent (cognitive creative) capacities and activities. Rather, the subject is able to do what it does only because it has had those abilities "bestowed upon it" already by being-in-the-world or what Gadamer (2004) calls tradition. So far, I have tried to illustrate that the language of passivity, drawn from phenomenology, can provide us with a vocabulary with which to talk about pre-decisions, pre-reflective awareness, non-opportunity (possibility) practice, pre-understanding and unintended responsibility that is not central to most entrepreneurial theories.

In order to improve theorizing and make the field of entrepreneurial studies more relevant to entrepreneurial practice, I think we would do better to speculate more about how different framings (becoming-in-being or Being-in-becoming; decision-in-place or place-in-decision; passivity-in-activity or activity-in-passivity) lead to various types of phenomena. Such a positive speculation may challenge (unarticulated) views and (perhaps pre-reflective) commitments regarding the nature of the world (ontological), the possibility of knowing (epistemological), and the methods of knowledge acquisition (methodology).

One central question is, could becoming and Being, decision-making and dwelling, activity and passivity be considered not as mutual repulsive aspects of entrepreneurial life, but as being in a more "balanced" and seamless transition (more on this in chapter 6.1).

References

Ahl, H. (2002). *The making of the female entrepreneur: A discourse analysis of research texts on women's entrepreneurship*, Jönköping International Business School, Dissertation Series, No. 15, Sweden.

Aldrich, H. & Cliff, J. (2003). The pervasive effects of family on entrepreneurship: Toward a family embeddedness perspective. *Journal of Business Venturing*, 18(5), 573–596.

Alvarez, S. (2005). *Theories of Entrepreneurship: Alternative Assumptions and the Study of Entrepreneurial Action*. Hanover: Now Publishers.

Bakhtin, M. (1981). *The dialogical imagination. Four essays by M. M Bakthin*. Holquist, C. (ed.). Austin TX: University of Texas.

Bass, F. M. (1969). A new product growth for model consumer durables. *Management Science*, 50, 1825–1832.

Boutaiba, S. (2004). Moment in time. In D. Hjorth & C. Steyaert (eds.), *Narrative and Discursive Approaches in Entrepreneurship: A Second Movement in Entrepreneurship Book*. Cheltenham: Edward Elgar Publishing. 22–56.

Buchanan, J. M. & Vanberg, V. J. (1991). The market as a creative process. *Economics and Philosophy*, 7, 167–186.

Busenitz, L. W. & Barney, J. W. (1997). Differences between entrepreneurs and managers in large organizations: Biases and heuristics in strategic decision-making. *Journal of Business Venturing*, 12(6), 9–30.

Cai, L., Guo, Y. & Liu, F. (2017). Effectuation, exploratory learning and new venture performance: Evidence from China. *Journal of Small Business Management*, 55(3), 388–403.

Camerer, C. & Lovallo, D. (1999). Overconfidence and excess entry: An experimental approach. *The American Economic Review*, 89(1), 306–318.

Churchill, N. C. & Lewis, V. L. (1983). The five stages of small business growth. *Harvard Business Review*, 61(3), 30–50.

Companys, Y. E. & McMullen, J. S. (2007). Strategic entrepreneurs at work: The nature, discovery, and exploitation of entrepreneurial opportunities. *Small Business Economics*, 28(4), 301–322.

Cooke, S. & Slack, N. (1984). *Making Management Decisions*. London: Prentice-Hall International.

Cosgel, M. (1996). Metaphors: Stories and the entrepreneur in economics. *History of Political Economy*, 28(1), 57–76.

Deleuze, G. (1995). *Negotiations. 1972–1990*. New York: Columbia University Press.

Dutta, D. & Crossan, M. (2005). The nature of entrepreneurial opportunities: Understanding the process using the 4I organizational learning framework. *Entrepreneurship: Theory and Practice*, 29(4), 425–449.

Eckhardt, J. T. & Shane, S. A. (2003). Opportunities and entrepreneurship. *Journal of Management*, 29(3), 333–349.

Fiet, J. O. (1996). The informational basis of entrepreneurial discovery. *Small Business Economics*, 419–430.

Fleming, D. (2001). Narrative leadership: Using the power of stories. *Strategy and Leadership*, 29(4), 2–16.

Fletcher, D. & Watson, T. (2006). Entrepreneurship, shifting life orientations and social change in the countryside. In C. Steyaert & D. Hjort (eds.), *Entrepreneurship as Social Change: A Third Movements in Entrepreneurship Book*. Cheltenham: Edward Elgar Publishing. 145–164.

Forlani, D. & Mullins, J. W. (2000). Perceived risks and choices in entrepreneurs' new venture decisions. *Journal of Business Venturing*, 15, 305–322.

Foss, L. (2003). Going against the grain . . . Construction of entrepreneurial identity through narratives. In D. Hjorth & C. Steyaert (eds.), *Narrative and Discursive Approaches in Entrepreneurship: A Second Movement in Entrepreneurship Book*. Cheltenham: Edward Elgar Publishing. 80–104.

Gadamer, H. G. (2004). *Truth and Method*. London: Continuum International Publishing Group Ltd.

Gartner, W. B. (2001). Is there an elephant in entrepreneurship? Blind assumptions in theory development. *Entrepreneurship Theory and Practice*, 25(4), 27–39.

Gartner, W. B., Carter, N. M. & Hills, G. E. (2003). The language of opportunity. In C. Steyaert & D. Hjorth (eds.), *New Movements in Entrepreneurship*. London: Edward Elgar Publishing. 103–124.

Gergen, K. J. (1999). *An invitation to social construction*. Thousand Oaks, CA: Sage Publishing.

Gustafsson, V. (2006). *Entrepreneurial Decision-Making: Individuals, Tasks and Cognitions*. Cheltenham: Edward Elgar Publishing.

Heidegger, M. (1960). *Sein und Zeit*. Tübingen: Max Niemeyer.

Heidegger, M. (1962). *Being and Time*. New York: Harper & Row Publishers.

Heidegger, M. (1978). *Poetry, Language, Thought*. New York: Harper Collins.

Hjorth, D. & Johannisson, B. (2009). Learning as an entrepreneurial process. *Revue de l'Entrepreneuriat*, 8(2), 57–78.

Hjorth, D. & Steyaert, C. (2004). *Narrative and Discursive Approaches in Entrepreneurship: A Second Movement in Entrepreneurship Book*. Cheltenham: Edward Elgar Publishing.

Johansson, A. W. (2004). Narrating the entrepreneur. *International Small Business Journal*, 22, 273–293.

Lévesque, M. & MacCrimmon, K. R. (1997). On the interaction of time and money invested in new ventures. *Entrepreneurship, Theory and Practice*, 22(2), 89–110.

Lévesque, M. & Schade, C. (2005). Intuitive optimizing: Experimental findings on time allocation decisions with newly formed ventures. *Journal of Business Venturing*, 20(3), 313–342.

Macann, C. (2007). Being and becoming. *Philosophy Now*, 61, 20–23.

Mantere, S., Aula, P., Schildt, H. & Vaara, E. (2013). Narrative attributions of narrative failure. *Journal of Business Venturing*, 28(4), 459–479.

March, J. G. & Simon, H. A. (1966). *Organizations*. New York: John Wiley and Sons.

McBride, R., Wuebker, R. & Grant, J. (2003). *The ontology of entrepreneurial opportunity*. Academy of Management Annual Meeting Proceedings (1), 16582–16582.

Mitchell, R. K., Busenitz, L., Lant, T., McDougall, P. P., Morse, E. A. & Smith, B. J. (2002). Toward a theory of entrepreneurial cognition rethinking the people side of entrepreneurship research. *Entrepreneurship Theory and Practice*, 27(2), 93–104.

Morris, M. (1998). *Entrepreneurial Intensity Sustainable Advantages for Individuals, Organizations, and Societies*. Westport, CT: Quorum Books.

Mukhi, S., Hampton, D. & Barnwell, N. (1988). *Australian Management*. Sydney, NSW: McGraw-Hill.

Mullins, J. W. & Forlani, D. (2005). Missing the boat or sinking the boat: A study of new venture decision making. *Journal of Business Venturing*, 20(1), 47–69.

Perren, L. & Ram, M. (2004). Case study method in small business and entrepreneurial research: Mapping boundaries and perspectives. *International Small Business Journal*, 22(1), 83–104.

Read, S., Song, M. & Smit, W. (2009). A meta-analytic review of effectuation and venture performance. *Journal of Business Venturing*, 24(6), 573–587.

Sarasvathy, S. D. (2001). Causation and effectuation: Toward a theoretical shift from economic inevitability to entrepreneurial contingency. *The Academy of Management Review*, 26(2), 243–264.

Sarasvathy, S. D. (2003). Entrepreneurship as a science of the artificial. *Journal of Economic Psychology*, 24, 203–220.

Sarasvathy, S. D. (2004). Making it happen: Beyond theories of the firm to theories of firm design. *Entrepreneurship Theory and Practice*, Winter, 519–531.

Sarasvathy, S. D. (2008). *Effectuation: Elements of Entrepreneurial Expertise*. Cheltenham: Edward Elgar Publishing.

Sarasvathy, S. D., Dew, N., Velamuri, S. R. & Venkataraman, S. (2003). Three views of entrepreneurial opportunity. In Z. J. Acs & D. B. Audretsch (eds.), *Handbook of Entrepreneurship Research: An Interdisciplinary Survey and Introduction*. Dordrecht, The Netherlands: Kluwer, 141–160.

Schade, C. & Burmeister-Lamp, K. (2009). Experiments on entrepreneurial decision making: A different lens through which to look at entrepreneurship. *Foundations and Trends in Entrepreneurship*, 5(2), 81–134.

Shane, S. A. (2003). *A General Theory of Entrepreneurship: The Individual-Opportunity Nexus*. Cheltenham: Edward Elgar Publishing.

Shane, S. A. & Venkataraman, S. (2000). The promise of entrepreneurship as a field of research. *Academy of Management Review*, 25, 217–226.

Shepherd, D. A. (2011). Multilevel entrepreneurship research: Opportunities for studying entrepreneurial decision making. *Journal of Management*, 37(2), 412–420.

Short, J. C., Ketchen, D. J., Shook, C. L. & Duan Ireland, R. (2010). The concept of "opportunity" in entrepreneurship research: Past accomplishments and future challenges. *Journal of Management*, 36(1), 40–65.

Simon, M. & Houghton, S. M. (2002). The relationship among biases, misperceptions, and the introduction of pioneering products examining differences in venture decision contexts. *Entrepreneurship Theory and Practice*, 27(2), 105–125.

Smolka, K. M., Verheul, I. & Burmeister-Lamp, K. (2015). *Successful entrepreneurs do both: Effectuation and causation, and the relation with firm performance.* Academy of Management Proceedings, 1.

Somers, M. (1994). The narrative constitution of identity: A relational and network approach. In *Theory and Practice*, 23, 605–699.

Steyaert, C. (1995). *Perpetuating entrepreneurship through dialogue.* Doctoral dissertation. Kathdike Universiteit Leuven, Leuven.

Steyaert, C. (1997). Human, all too human resource management: Constructing the subject in HRM. *Papers in Organization*, No. 28, Copenhagen.

Steyaert, C. (1998). A qualitative methodology for process studies of entrepreneurship: Creating local knowledge through stories. *International Studies of Management and Organisation*, 27(3), 13–33.

Steyaert, C. (2003). *Entrepreneurship: In between what? On the "frontier" as a discourse of entrepreneurship research.* Best Paper Proceedings, Academy of Management, 1–6.

Steyaert, C. (2004). The prosaics of entrepreneurship. In C. Steyaert & D. Hjorth (eds.), *New Movements in Entrepreneurship*. Cheltenham: Edward Elgar Publishing. 8–21.

Steyaert, C. & Hjorth, D. (2003). Entrepreneurship beyond (a new) economy. In C. Steyaert & D. Hjorth (eds.), *New Movements in Entrepreneurship*. Cheltenham: Edward Elgar Publishing. 286–303.

Timmons, J., Spinelli, S. & Zacharakis, A. (2005). *How to Raise Capital*. New York: McGraw-Hill.

Van de Ven, A., Angle, H. & Poole, M. (2000). *Research on the Management of Innovation: The Minnesota Studies*. New York: Oxford University Press.

Venkataraman, S. (1997). The distinctive domain of entrepreneurship research. *Advances in Entrepreneurship, Firm Emergence and Growth*, 3, 119–138.

Young, J. (2000). What is dwelling? The homelessness of modernity and the worlding of the world. In M. Wrathall & J. Malpass (eds.), *Heidegger, Authenticity and Modernity*. Cambridge: MIT Press. 187–204.

Part 2

Towards a Theory of "Nothing" in Entrepreneurial Practice

3 Introduction on Heidegger and Philosophy of Being and Nothing

This chapter outlines key terms relevant to a theory of nothing in Heidegger's philosophy. We refer to concepts such as Being-there, Being-in-the-world, technology, nothing, time/place/dwelling and projection. Rather than presenting all the relevant potential terms, we offer a selection of what a theory of nothing may include, while recognizing that this sample is limited.

Practice and everyday meaning play key roles in Martin Heidegger's (1889–1976) philosophy. Heidegger's initial academic studies in theology gradually kindled his interest in hermeneutics and phenomenology. The year 1927 marked Heidegger's breakthrough as a philosopher, along with the publication of the first part of *Being and Time*, which provided the basis for an obstinately etymology-oriented philosophy that seeks to deconstruct the history of metaphysics. In brief, Heidegger's strategy involves investigating the possibility conditions for having lost the meaning of being ever since the ancient Greek conception of Being. In other words, he was particularly interested in delving more deeply into the conditions that have enabled this historic process. Heidegger fears that technology and modern science will contribute to an even greater extent to Being's oblivion, or that we will live in "forgottenness" in relation to the mystery of being (*Seinvergessenheit*). The establishment of the key term *Dasein* (being there/existence) represents a quest for a fruitful alternative approach to the mystery of being. *Dasein* denotes a dimension in a special relationship to existence that potentially makes it more suitable than many traditional terms (cognition/reason, consciousness, subject, object etc.) to encompass the ultimate possibility of existence, or existential possibility. Heidegger seems to have an urge to free himself of traditional terms or suppositions, and of mundane terminology, so that he is able, in a phenomenological manner, to approach the phenomena themselves (*die Sache selbst*). Through another key term—Being in the world (*In-der-Welt-Sein*)—the phenomena themselves can be expressed in the modern world.

A modern entrepreneurship and business practice may be a matter of a much too strong visibility and transparency—a basic way of being in the world. This is not a panoptic visualization making everything visible to the outer eye. It is a transparency that is transparent not only for others, but also for oneself. Both the carpenter and the entrepreneur, with Heidegger's (2007) thinking, may run the risk of turning the world into an object for producing things. This is a mode of practice that in the end recoils and strikes the subject and the entrepreneur himself, because it perceives itself as a thing amongst things—a practice/world that is not alarming in its nature, but that is even worse due to a dual transparence that has lost its own self-reflection.

With Heidegger, it is possible to rediscover the meaning of the question as to how our modes of usage and self-understanding can be rediscovered and challenged. Heidegger finds a contrast to this transparent self-understanding and the temporary distance in a modern attempt to continuously distance oneself from, dominate and control nature (cf. Descartes and Bacon). The modern era (its quest for power) turns people and nature into materials for their projects in such a way that Heidegger seeks an alternative type of reason (Denken)—a type of thinking that can be placed in context with the issue of the meaning of being. This can be more closely accounted for through the application of terms such as being-there and being-in-the-world.

3.1   Being-There, Being-in-the-World

For Heidegger (1962), the threshold to a deeper understanding of being or existence is encumbered with the issue of the meaning of existence altogether. It is worthwhile to note that the manner in which the question of the meaning of existence is treated may be read as a certain type of entrepreneurial philosophy. In his work *Being and Time*, Heidegger (1962) takes as his point of departure that being-there (Dasein) is the only form of existence/being that can provide an answer as to the meaning of being, and being-there (Dasein) therefore has a special status. What is it that is so special with being-there and why is it distinguished from other entities? Heidegger (1962) responds:

> Dasein is a being that occurs not only among beings. Dasein is ontically distinguished by the fact that, in its very Being, that Being is an issue for it. . . . This being is distinguished by the fact that it is opened for this being by virtue of and through its being. . . . Dasein's ontic distinction lies in the fact that it is ontological.

(p. 14)

Dasein can be regarded as an ontically privileged dimension in relation to other entities in terms of access to and understanding of Being/existence. This means that ontic entities in the field of entrepreneurial research such as risk, uncertainty, mindset and personality traits cannot comprehend (and realize) existence in the same fundamental way as Dasein. Nor is it true that ontic conceptions such as the person and the entrepreneur can be equated with Dasein existence; they can only be confronted with themselves. Such an existential confrontation does not always occur, and Dasein sometimes becomes a concealed condition for Being in the World. Thus, it is a case of Dasein's encouraging an anticipation of its own existence. This is a basic, inherent and decisive trait for (genuine) human beingness, according to Heidegger (2007). Being "there" has a special meaning because "Dasein" means to relate to a type of existence/being by anticipating one's own existence in the uniqueness of the moment. Being present in the "here and now" in unique isolation, "there" can therefore challenge existence and jeopardize existence. Existence or Dasein can put oneself at risk, conceal and open oneself. To borrow Heidegger's (2007) well-known example of the hammer, we engage ourselves in the world in a theoretically distanced way when we strike our fingers holding the nail rather than the nail itself; or when we repair the shaft of the hammer; or when we simply lift the hammer out of the toolbox to examine it as a thing that is called a hammer. Every perception of the type "the hammer is too heavy" or "the hammer is too small" is an expression of a theoretical understanding that can open for another way of applying and understanding the hammer. Likewise, the entrepreneur can understand himself in another way through changing market conditions, new business networks, new clients, lacking technical solutions, where the usual "tools" are no longer relevant.

A challenge relating to Dasein's own existence can lie in the way we understand. It is possible to claim that existence can be transformed and realized on the basis of its being part of other usage contexts. In such a perspective, one might say that Dasein will always have unending existential potentials to change the attributes of the hammer and entrepreneurial conditions or to create new and better tools by which, thereby, to change itself. Existential questions can be posed only based on Dasein as a way of existence, and it is only based on Dasein that existential questions *are not* always posed. From this perspective it is possible to see that different forms, or modi, of Dasein exist. Heidegger (2007) writes of two ways that Dasein practically interacts with objects in the world. One way can be termed practical understanding (*Zuhanden*) and the other distanced theoretical understanding (*Vorhanden*). Both are basic ways of being in the world (In-der-Welt-Sein). A practical understanding, however, has a tendency to lean more towards Dasein. Heidegger (2007) does not make provisions for *asserting* this in his project, but he tries to show us how the way we most often meet the world is of a basically practical nature determined by a (pre-ontological) understanding of the specific tool and tool-ness ("*Das Zeug*") that is suitable to execute the task at hand. A round of practical understanding concerning tools (including everything from the physical thing to linguistic signs), whereby one understands, for example, how a hammer is used denotes a fundamental familiarity with the world. The point is that it is not possible *to understand* a hammer or an entrepreneurial practice merely by knowing what one looks like, its potential or how it can be used, because such a knowledgeable appraisal must depend on Dasein's always already understanding its context of utilization (practical understanding). Heidegger (1977) describes one variant of our already understood or careful treatment of tools in his essay *The Question Concerning Technology*.

3.2   Being-in-the-World as Technology and Enframing

For Heidegger (1977), technology is primarily not merely one of several human domains, but rather a widespread understanding of ourselves and being. One can say that technology is the form in which being in our time is manifested, concealed or enframed within. Our ways of being within technology, whether it be in the family, religion, education, academic life or communication, are in a way enframed and made ready for use (mobilized). In this respect, Heidegger (1977) speaks of a system (*Enframing*) as an all-encompassing view that describes a mode of existence. The key point is that Heidegger (1977) points out that our relations with technology render that which is procured as having a value only by virtue of its being procurable. Does this, then, result in everything in existence becoming instruments for us, and that we, entrepreneurs and researchers, are "masters of the situation" in the age of technology? In the event that we believe we are "masters of situations", then technology and our procurements/arrangements threaten to get the upper hand over the nature of thought and language, Heidegger says (1977).

In his later work *The Question Concerning Technology*,Heidegger (1977) states that the essence (*Wesen*) of modern technology lies in *Enframing* (*Gestell*) or revealing. This is challenging and ordering, and includes being reminded of and conceiving how the phenomenon of technology comes to be present and endures. Heidegger (1977) argues that the traditional ways of conceiving technology are inadequate. Neither the anthropological view that technology is one form of human activity among many (e.g. including also *praxis* and *theoria*), nor the instrumentalist view that technology is a neutral tool, a means to an end that can be calculated and controlled by conscious human direction, grasps the essence of modern technology. The distinctive mode of technology always stands prior to any conscious act taken on the basis of what is already revealed. Heidegger (1977, pp. 17, 26) states that;

> Everywhere everything is ordered to stand by, to be immediately at hand, indeed to stand there just so that it may be on call for a further ordering. Whatever is ordered about in this way has its own standing. We call it the standing-reserve [Bestand]". . . . Thus . . . "Where Enframing holds sway, the regulating and securing of standing in reserve marks all. They no longer even allow their own fundamental characteristic of revealing to appear. . . . Thus the challenging Enframing conceals not only a former way of revealing or bringing-forth, but it conceals itself and with it that wherein unconcealment, e.g., truth, comes to pass.

That is to say, man, entrepreneurs and researchers should apply technology not only as an instrument at hand, but as a way of revealing. Heidegger (1977) states that metaphysics "represents" being as beings. This kind of representation is a displacement in being where beings are no longer experienced as they are but as things determined at one's disposal. In this determination beings are set aside, as a standing by (*Bestand*) in which time and space are abstracted and have no real, ontological bearing. Heidegger (1977) refers to this dislocation as "the standing-reserve", a spatial determination that distorts time and in turn affects how we consider time and being. One example is the understanding of clock time. It is essentially a spatial relation to time in which temporality itself is conceived as a sequence of nows. The nows determine time in a specific way that, according to Heidegger (1977), reinforces the technological understanding of progress. Time is repeated and secures its mastery over nature. This is an interpretation in which time itself is subordinated to the desire to gain control. Here, the repetition necessary in experimentation is a manner of flattening down time so that it can be repeated, which makes time conform to a series of tests that can assure us of certain results or a method by which to attain such results. These results are value determinations and such determinations stand before, and then subsequently as, the presencing of being. It is about getting things stored and kept on "standby" for future use, manipulation and ordering. Modern technology, for example business/entrepreneurial tools (i.e. business models, techniques of analysis of innovativeness, competitive advantages, firm based resources etc.) takes what is, transforms it and keeps it in "standing reserve" until it is wanted. Heidegger (1962, 1977, 1993) asks how it is that we see things as we do when man is cut off from that mysterious ground of all that comes to presence. That is to say, Dasein (self-understanding) "owns up" to the *nihil*, the abyss, present within itself, i.e. the nothingness encountered within the meaningful horizon of its own being. The grounds for what is are in the groundless ground (nothingness) of Dasein as understanding what is, through transcendence. Transcendence is the fundamental aspect of Dasein on the basis of which it can relate to any other being (*MitDasein*), i.e. in the entrepreneurial team, competitors, partners. It is being-in-the-world, as the basic way in which Dasein is in the world, as disclosive, and as temporal. Transcendence precedes every possible mode of activity, i.e. it is prior to any practical or theoretical mode of understanding the world, prior to all behaviour (Heidegger 1962).

3.3   Narrowing the Scope: On Theory of Nothing

In this section I draw upon Heidegger's texts (1962, 1977, 1993) *Being and Time* and *What Is Metaphysics?* to show some aspects of how the "Theory of nothing" can be a condition for existence and reveal itself for an entrepreneurial practice and applicable or technological (research) paradigm. However, it is important to keep in mind the latest section and how the "macro" conditions of Nothing may reveal and unfold themselves, i.e. how technology (Gestell) influences entrepreneurial practice and research. In the empirical vignettes, (chapters 6–7), the relations between technology/ applied paradigm and nothing will be explored further.

Moreover, due to this negligence of the meaning of Being, man (the "who" of everyday Dasein is Das Man or man) has lost almost all his connections with Being and lives now in a technical and artificial world (Heidegger 1962, 1977, 1993). That is to say, man has lost his *ground* and is not-at-home anymore. By taking the question of Being as the clue, Heidegger (1962) is concerned about the Being behind all beings or entities, which can be grasped by the self-understanding of *Dasein* (human being). The human being (Dasein) is always already (being-in-the-world) in a process of opening entities into our world involvement. In this way, we categorically perceive entities *as* entities either as themselves or as something they are not, but always for-the-sake of some circumspective activity (Heidegger 1977). It is being-in-the-world (In-der-Welt-Sein) and this perception "for-the-sake" of which also constitutes nothing or the experience of nothingness.

3.4 Nothingness and the Experience of "Nothing"

Why are there beings rather than nothing? This is the question Heidegger (1993) asserts in his famous *What Is Metaphysics?* According to Heidegger (1993), the way we encounter this question is essential. By encounter he does not mean merely to hear and read about it as an interrogative formulation but to ask the question, to bring it about, i.e. to feel its inevitability. It is important to know that nothing or nothingness is not the void brought about by imagining that everything that exists is gone, and it is not the result of the logical act of universal negation. The question can be posed as a whole and also from the essential position of existence (Dasein). In this way, Heidegger (1993) challenges the authority of logic and its prime representative science. Science as technology or the applied paradigm only deals with something, and it accepts nothing of the nothing, according to Heidegger (1993). Rhetorically he asks, how can the nothing be tested, verified? Science does not want to trouble itself with the nothing. Science, says Heidegger (1993, p. 84), "wishes to know nothing of the nothing". As Richard Polt (1999, p. 123) comments:

> Heidegger starts by emphasizing science's "submission to beings themselves". Good chemists, economists or historians all have this in common: they want to know what is the case, what is true and only that. They are devoted to beings alone—and nothing else.

It is this assumption of science that Heidegger rejected in his elaboration of the nothing (*das Nichts*). Science is impotent to describe the nothing, and science, in expressing its own proper essence, never calls upon the nothing for help (Heidegger 1993). Nothing and the world are intertwined; they exist as the shadow in the presence of light. The world can be understood as nothing. The world is the nothing that originally (*nihil originarium*) temporalizes itself and simply arises in and with the temporalizing (*Zeitigung*). We may call the world the original nothing (*nihil originarium*). Moreover, in *What Is Metaphysics?* Heidegger develops another theme that is not seen in *Being and Time*, namely the relationship between being and nothing. He states that in "the being of beings the nihilation (*Nichten*) of nothing occurs" (Heidegger 1993, p. 91). Heidegger takes nothing as to be equivalent to being. This equalization neatly captures the basic meaning of nothing in Heidegger's usage, namely, as something experienced by Dasein's Angst, equivalent to being, and functioning through negation and withdrawal. The most extensive discussion of nothing is found in Heidegger's *Being and Time*. The work illustrates how nothing is revealed and experienced in *Angst* (I use the German term Angst instead of the English translation "anxiety", because the concept of Angst refers more to a human condition than "anxiety" which may be more associated with a psycho-pathological disorder).

How, then, can we approach the nothing? Heidegger (1962) opens the window to the nothing through Angst. He describes ways in which a person can encounter nothingness, and thereby takes hold of his or her existence authentically. As the critical philosopher Critcley (2009, N.P.) put it, using maritime terms:

> I like to think about this in maritime terms. Inauthentic life in the world is completely bound up with things and other people in a kind of "groundless floating"—the phrase is Heidegger's. Everyday life in the world is like being immersed in the sea and drowned by the world's suffocating banality. Anxiety is the experience of the tide going out, the seawater draining away, revealing a self stranded on the strand, as it were. Anxiety is that basic mood when the self first distinguishes itself from the world and becomes self-aware.

Most of the time, perhaps not intentionally, the entrepreneurial world (both entrepreneurs and researchers) treat people as what Heidegger terms "Equipment" (*das Zeug*) or as if they were tools within the applied paradigm, rather than Beings in themselves. This contributes to not being able to be self-aware through nothing before *the tide is receding*.

The "saving" for this lack of nothingness lies in insights not only from poetry but perhaps art. It is works of art that will help us to step back from ourselves and appreciate the independent existence of other people and things.

Heidegger (2001) in *The Origin of the Work of Art* elaborated this idea in the course of a discussion of a painting by Van Gogh of a pair of peasant shoes. In a short and simplified manner, Heidegger offers the following interpretation: In our everyday lives, we don't pay much attention to shoes; they are merely another bit of "equipment" that we need to get by. But when they are presented to us on a canvas, we may notice them, as if for the first time, for their own sake. The same might happen within entrepreneurial practice (including researchers) when confronted by other bits of the natural and the man-made world (this can be determined neither a priori nor by any predictable circumstances) represented not literally by great artists, but by considering customers' behaviour, everyday products as not everlasting and natural. Thanks to art/entrepreneurship/innovation, we might feel a new kind of "might be" or "impossible possibilities" for Being that lie beyond the current entrepreneurial mind and (self-)understanding.

However, this is not accomplished by simply doing a cognitive exercise. According to Heidegger (1993), it is (only) *the feeling* of Angst that genuinely reveals nothingness, i.e. the possible non-being of everything that I am. This experience is always possible for Dasein (human understanding) and it does not need an unusual event to arouse it, because, "its sway is as thorough going as its possible occasionings are trivial. It is always ready, though it only seldom springs, and we are snatched away and left hanging" (Heidegger 1993, p. 93). That is to say, Angst/anxiety does not need darkness, helplessness and despair. It can arise in the most everyday situations: sitting at a café distractedly reading a book and overhearing conversations, one is suddenly seized by the feeling of meaninglessness, by the radical distinction between yourself and the world in which you find yourself. With this experience of Angst, being-there (with nothing) is individualized and becomes self-aware. Angst should not be equated with a negative experience. Instead it can be understood and seized as a precondition for waking up and being-there. In ordinary everyday life we tend to be locked into routine, and being preoccupied by practical tasks (*Zuhanden*), and busy with their execution, we rarely question the sense of the whole system of cares, goals and activities. Angst relieves us of the automatized world and enables us to make our own personal decisions. Angst can be the means to becoming our own selves. By prompting us to become genuine individuals, it can make our lives authentic. This Angst is a way of turning the mind away from logic towards questions without answers. Moreover, it is not possible to pursue Angst and nothing, because neither can be grasped through conscious deliberate intention. For Heidegger (1962), this meditative and transforming "step-back" can allow us to encounter the world in a genuinely new way, and allow us to become attuned to the openness or nothingness pervading all things. As such, nothing is a kind of being-in-the-world even if we are "stepping-back", or more precisely, it is possible to understand the world as a dwelling place with a peculiar concept of time.

3.5 "The Dwelling Place" as Ethical Construct and Perception of Time

Heidegger (2007) traces the etymological meaning of the word *ethics*, i.e. The Greek ethos, which—aside from the notion of habitual character—can also mean *the place where we dwell*. For Heidegger (1977), it is not essential that we line up rules for rigid application (*Ge-stell*), but instead that a person's Dasein (sometimes) finds its way to the place in existence/Being's clearing, opening or truth. It is only after reaching this dwelling place that one experiences durability. This durability is closely linked with the fact that human life is lived in time and that the person and entrepreneur can temporalize time. Time no longer exists in this respect under the perspective of eternity (theology), nor can it be reduced to a physicist's numerical determination of it. It is the moment and the place, both as object and subject, that enable one to understand time based on time itself, the lived life "here and now", and not time understood either as a divinely contingent eternity or as a homogeneous temporal current that can be quantified. In this sense, it is to no avail to avoid wasting time or taking one's time to do something. A reservation against spending time and pursuing a pastime imply that time should belong to us rather than we to it. To remain outside time and temporality thereby puts us (Dasein) at risk of losing touch with meaningful places to be. Consequently, life no longer gives any response. To look at one's watch in an attempt to discover the instant as if the instant is one of a series of nows running through present time, that is, to see the instant at a single point, is the wrong "strategy" and way of being if one is to be part of time's homogeneous horizon. It is only when the horizon encompassing what was, what is and what will be rests on Being in the World that a scope of action can be created for the determined (entrepreneur). This can open for restoring Dasein's meaning in a complete time horizon.

Based on the dwelling place, Dasein regains control of itself from a "blind" or a practical understanding and responds to its place or its Situation. The answer involves choosing oneself through resolution, where the moment is the glance of decision in which the full situation for action opens and remains open (Heidegger 2007). To conceptualize time as the meaning of Dasein, the moment, is regarded by Heidegger (2007) as a possibility condition for existence. The choice must be made and the decision must be enabled. The most important thing is *how* this occurs, that is, based on a future, realized existential task, and not what the content of Dasein is associated with. This *how* is essential because a genuine moment cannot be predetermined, and because the dwelling place may feel incomprehensibly foreign in its awfulness. In this context, Heidegger (2007) says that "Terribleness is the basic mode of being in the world, although it is ordinarily concealed" (p. 259). To be on foreign and terrible ground without being able to use familiar tools may put existence at risk and thereby open for a new scope of action.

For example, a carpenter's or entrepreneur's existence (Dasein) can be challenged and realized on the basis of an unsatisfactory/transparent use of tools, which entails other (theoretical) assessments, decisions and appraisals, before a new use and a new appraisal can again be introduced in the homely/confidential carpenter and entrepreneur practice. Theoretical understanding is brought home. In the carpenter's world, the carpenter is at home in a dwelling place. In the entrepreneur's world, the entrepreneur is at home in a dwelling place. In the same way, it is possible, for example, to speak of the carpenter's world, the entrepreneur's world etc., where familiarity in the use of tools is shown in such a way that one feels at home or "accommodates being" as a "dwelling place". The ethic therefore becomes a question of assessing which "dwelling places" we find ourselves in and at the same time offer strong resistance and show ever new potentials (of existence) that can be realized.

From the foregoing, it should be clear that Heidegger emphasizes the "placedness" and dwelling with which we engage in our day-to-day activities, at least, when we are immersed in what we are doing. It is impossible to be objective when one is totally involved with what one is doing. As noted before, this is completely antithetical to the scientific, rational view in which we are supposed to be at our best, to maintain a detached, dispassionate view of the world. Another pivotal aspect of the entrepreneurial world of Being and understanding of nothing is what is called projection.

3.6   Projection

Heidegger (1996, p. 136) asks the question:

> "Why does understanding always penetrate into possibilities according to all the essential dimension of what can be disclosed to it?" His direct answer is that "It is because the understanding has in itself the existential structure which we call 'projection'".

It is important to keep in mind that *Understanding* is an existential aspect; it is involved in the nature of *possibility* and it has the nature of *projection*. Projection thus means a sort of antecedent comprehending. This "projective" Understanding (*Sicht*) has access to both beings and Being (Dasein), that is to say, it moves in two ways:

a.   towards the *world* i.e. significance (as the totality of involvements) i.e., the understanding of (Zuhanden) entities or applicable objects within the world; This understanding may be compared to how entrepreneurs manipulate analytical tools, i.e. business plans without having any problem with doing so.

b.   towards the *for-the-sake-of-which* i.e. Dasein (being-there) gaining access to itself self-understanding. This may point towards how entrepreneurs at first might understand themselves and their business differently.

In other words, the *projecting* of the *understanding* has the *possibility* of developing itself; that is, the understanding has the possibility of referring back to itself, of "understanding itself". As such, being-there understands itself in terms of possibilities. Furthermore, the character of understanding as projection is such that the understanding does not grasp thematically that upon which it projects, that is to say, possibilities. Grasping it in such a manner would take away from what is projected its very character as a possibility, and would reduce it to the given contents which we have in mind; whereas projection throws before itself the possibility as possibility, and lets it *be* as such. As projecting, understanding is the kind of Being of Dasein in which it is its possibilities as possibilities.

To summarize this chapter, the notions of being-there, being-in-the-world, technology/applied paradigm, projection involve relinquishing the "automatized" and "practical" self-understanding (Dasein) which may hinder us from being open to possibilities, and hence to nothing. Entrepreneurship is often understood as the art of the new: new ventures, new companies, new products, innovations and so on. It would thus seem to be contradictory to speak about "nothing" and the importance of "a theory of Nothing" with regard to the constructive creation of new products, ventures and the like. Instead of embracing the oxymoronic and paradoxical nature of entrepreneurial nothingness, which considers entrepreneurial being and nothing as mutually exclusive aspects, I offer the view that it is a valid and useful addition and condition to the lexicon of entrepreneurial technology decision-making practices. It is incorrect to view "nothing" and entrepreneurial as being opposites. This applies equally to lay thinking and the very theory or essence of entrepreneurship. I will also claim that there is much to be gained or recalled from understanding a "theory of nothing". It is possible to rethink certain taken-for granted notions about what entrepreneurship consists of (technology, risk, opportunity etc.), and hence expand the notion of the entrepreneurial practice, research and theory (see chapter 6).

References

Critcley, S. (2007). *Very Little Almost Nothing: Death, Philosophy and Literature.* London: Routledge.

Heidegger, H. (1977). The question concerning technology. In W. Lovitt (ed.), *The Question Concerning Technology and Other Essays.* New York: Harper & Row Publishers.

Heidegger, M. (1962/2007). *Being and Time.* New York: Harper & Row Publishers.

Heidegger, M. (1993). Was ist Metaphysik?. In *M. Heidegger, Wegmarken, Gesamtausgabe.* (Trans.) V. Klostermann, English translation as (Heidegger 1993). Frankfurt: Vittorio Klostermann.

Heidegger, M. (1996). *Being and Time: A Translation of Sein und Zeit.* Albany, NY: State University of New York Press.

Heidegger, M. (2001). The Origin of the Work of Art. In M. Heidegger (ed.), *Poetry, Language, Thought.* New York: Perennial Classics. 15–86.

Polt, R. (1999). *Heidegger: An Introduction.* London: UCL Press.

4 Vignettes and Examples

In this chapter vignettes and examples from entrepreneurial research are presented in order to show the significance of "nothing" and the courses of events that take place when entrepreneurs become entrepreneurial. As mentioned earlier, not much Heideggerian-inspired entrepreneurial research exists (see Spinoza, Flores, and Dreyfus 1997), and even (phenomenological) existential and personal experience-oriented themes are rare (see Popp and Holt 2013). Research on entrepreneurial (Nothing) experience is even rarer, but can be found in some few dissertations; for example "For Love or Money: Understanding the Dynamics of Within-Family Finance Start-Up Enterprise" (Hancock 2013);[1] "How Do Metal Musicians Become Entrepreneurial?" (Hauge 2011).[2] It is only in Hancock's dissertation that the phrase Nothing and Angst is explicitly articulated. Hauge's (2011) dissertation uses terms from Heidegger (e.g. potential, actual, place, projecting etc.). In my opinion, all these sources provide rare but illuminating examples of Nothing in entrepreneurial practice, which makes it possible to trace some of the paths whereby entrepreneurs become entrepreneurial. In addition, using examples and (firsthand) data from research conducted by Rennemo and Åsvoll (2016),[3] it is possible to show so how experience and existential spheres and transformations among four entrepreneurs open up interpretations of Angst or "nothing practice".

Heidegger's concepts or aspects as headings/technology/applicable paradigm, Angst/Nothing and projection are used when presenting examples and research findings from these different sources. Under these headings, other terms are used such as dwelling places, time, being-there, being-in-the world (cf. chapter 3). However, this does not mean that each concept is an independent category that alone describes a phenomenon. Nor does it mean that Heidegger's concepts occur in a logical order in the phenomenon through which entrepreneurs undergo the experience of nothing and begin to act and re-invent entrepreneurial practice. It is important to note that these three aspects are phenomenological in nature. That is, they are about deep meanings and are not first and foremost psychological traits/attitudes or sociological manifestations (norms, roles etc.). They are something more and beyond that; they are based on a being-in-the-world, a life view and existence that rests on a reflective structure. The deep meanings may show how entrepreneurs understand themselves in a world representing ontological rather than ontic aspects of entrepreneurial practice.

I begin with an analysis of the perceived dominant condition of entrepreneurship conceptualized as Gestell/Technology/applicable paradigm. Technology describes how entrepreneurs relate to ready-to-hand, "applicable"/ tool-based and a sort of automatized practice, which in turn are relevant in the way they constitute their genuine understanding of the horizon of possibilities and opportunities. For this purpose, I think that Heidegger's concept of Gestell/technology is a relevant entrance for readers to become familiar with one of the modern conditions of entrepreneurial life, as it is perceived by researchers and entrepreneurs. Entrepreneurs, as human beings, are born and thrown into a complex world, where they have to learn to master skills and tools simply to be able to cope in the world. Gestell/technology thus influences entrepreneurs' understanding of opportunities, as well as their experiences and life-projects. It is in technology that entrepreneurial beings are introduced to tools (or equipment, in Heideggerian terms) and where tools become ready-to-hand, handy and "applicable".

4.1   Technology and the Applicable Paradigm

In Hauge's (2011) dissertation, three musicians (in the world-famous Norwegian metal music environment) are investigated in depth (phenomenological approach) and interviewed in order to analyse how they became entrepreneurial, i.e. the processes by which musicians become entrepreneurs. I have extracted some data and interpretations that may serve to illustrate the presence of aspects of the "theory of nothing". Here are some illustrations from the musicians' stories;

> The musicians were constantly asked for business plans and descriptions of market situations. Even though they tried to meet the support services' demand for draft project proposals Kjetil experienced that the consultants did not understand the objective nor motive of the musicians' planned business ventures. Instead of managing to penetrate the support services' codes for project planning and presentations, Kjetil and Terje were continually sent to knock on the next door within the public support service system. To me, it seems Kjetil is describing what it is like being caught in a vicious endless circle where the focus is always on securing endless investments for the future, and never using

the financial gains for present artistic purposes. This kind of focus does not encourage creativity.

(Hauge 2011, p. 86)

The focus seems sharp and intense on meeting demands for draft project proposals and planned business ventures. This "vicious endless circle" is perhaps underlined in the context of a drastic decrease in record sales caused by music consumers' illegal file sharing. Hauge (2011) continues when she asks Kjetil if marketing is one of the most challenging tasks;

> It is a lot of work. You have to follow possible business partners all over the world. In each country we signed two-year distribution contracts, one company in each country, and some of the distributors did a good job for us. But there are also companies that we have not fully exploited the potentials of the distribution contracts with because they were not interested in speaking with us. After two years with distributors, we wanted to continue collaborating with some of them, and keep them for the future. But it is also true that you get a totally new understanding of how market mechanisms work when you become involved in the industry's business relations. On top of all this, we were also supposed to get out and do good live jobs as well.
>
> (Hauge 2011, p. 87)

Marketing as a strategy is a kind of tool just waiting to be used, i.e. contracts to be signed and distributed. It seems the musicians are "caught" to look at the world as a set of resources and where the emphasis is on resource utilization or what in Heideggerian terms is technology (or Ge-stell).

In line with the marketing strategies and activity reported from musicians, it is possible to show the same technology with regard to the facilitated interaction among four entrepreneurs (cf. Rennemo and Åsvoll 2016). In the summaries of each entrepreneur during the interactions, they told about reactions and ideas they got from the group regarding their business and their role as managers. Here are some comments from three of the entrepreneurs:

Deborah: Your idea about spending a regular day on marketing activities, and involving a group of my employees in this, is something I'll take along with me. I think this is a good idea for us. (As a response to this, Anna comments and gives further advice on how to make plans for marketing activities and how to delegate and follow up. Deborah makes notes while Anna is speaking.)

Brenda: I realize that I need to focus more on project development and delegate the responsibility of handling them to some of my employees. My challenge is related to Deborah's, and her marketing activities. I need to find a structure for this and protect myself from the operational level.

These comments indicate that marketing activities at the operational level as technology is something that takes too much energy and focus and in the end should be delegated to and handled by someone else in the organization.

Much like entrepreneurial musicians and the four entrepreneurs, the entrepreneurial life within-family finance for a start-up enterprise is characterized by necessary and important "enablers" and activities which somehow are not favourable aspects (from the entrepreneurs' perspective). For example, take the perspective that beyond worldly things, beyond the rational return on investments,

> money really is an enabler, not for what it is . . . exactly, it's not an end in itself, it's a way to get to where you want (P12R20).
>
> (Hancock 2013, p. 161)

The shared focus here, even if it concerns such different things as the need for funding or marketing, seems to be about what is almost at some point in time inevitable or perhaps applicable. There seems to be an understanding engaged largely with unreflective ready-to-hand activity within the applicable paradigm. In other words, "It's already there, just order it" (i.e. funding and marketing).

Summary

Diving still deeper, running up against the ontology of entrepreneurship, its underlying theory of reality, this ontology can at this moment be summed up at this moment with the phrase, "something is already there and applicable, just order!" That is to say, the world is a perfect prototype. The entrepreneurial way makes perfect sense when applied to business plans, contracts, marketing and funding. Applied to social reality, however, it has severe ontological implications. Treating entrepreneurial reality or world as raw materials to be ordered may change the way we think of it. The world emerges as a neutral field of resources that can be moved about, uncoupled, recoupled and exploited. It's as if the world were just a one-dimensional field of object-resources where it is more difficult to see inherent value and nothing. In principle, everything is manipulable. Are they really so simple that entrepreneurs need only to go do it and fix it (i.e. business plans, funds and marketing)? Or, it is possible to claim that entrepreneurs in pre-decision moments and dwelling places believe that something can always be better which is not already there, and that *nothing* is ever complete.

4.2   Angst and Nothing in Entrepreneurial Life

First it is important to note that nothing always exists, even though it may conceal itself in everyday life. In phenomenological terms, nothing relies on absence for its presence. One of these "hiding" places is called a dwelling place or "the experience or feeling of being 'at home' in one's world. To dwell is to live a life that is informed by the experience of the place in which one lives as a dwelling-place, a homeland" (Young 2000, p. 194). In a vignette from the dissertation written by Hauge (2011), a dwelling place and the experience of homeland is described:

> The main aim of acting out this attitude was too promote a mystical myth about In the Woods. Still, the band was surprised by the success of this way of meeting the music audience. The bandleader, Jan Kenneth had normally controlled the profile and attitude that was presented to the press. At the time, Jan Kenneth had a preference for and an interest in being out in the forest where he tried to live in harmony with nature. He found inspiration in the forest, lighting a small fire and creating a good atmosphere. The forest inspired creativity and the place around the fire was ideal for philosophizing and exchanging thoughts. This is also a lifestyle or attitude promoted in media;
>
>> What we tried to do when we made music was to recreate our daily life in the music. The first album was a composition about the relationship between human beings and nature. It was very much a philosophical rumination, and was niche oriented. I was more on the love and peace side.
>>
>> (Hauge 2011, p. 76)
>
> For musicians, the life project is their artistic universe put together by their talent, creativity and desire to create outcomes such as new songs, albums, live shows, festivals, sound studios, and record companies. The life project is not only about creating a job, but it is about creating a musicians' life.
>
> (Hauge 2011, p. v)

In dwelling places (such as the forest), nothing is normally below the surface or is reluctant to reveal itself. This is not always the case, because sometimes dwelling places arise. Several vignettes from Hancock's (2013) dissertation indicate the presence of Angst and nothing. First the presence of Nothing among family entrepreneurs is motivated by trying to avoid it, even though nothing is more present than completely absent:

Vignette

The drive that some of the participants showed to overcome the Angst of not achieving their aims was often expressed as a feeling or belief. It was a level of determination that overcomes the primary fear of the ability to repay the money that is provided by their family.

> So you've got a belief which reduces the feeling of obligation because you know it's just going to happen. I think belief (is the) most important thing in business, in business success. . . . [B]elieve in what you do.

The drive to achieve something (avoiding Nothingness) was evident from a participant who was very aware that he needed a change in career (Hancock 2013, p. 164).

This vignette is indicative of the phenomenon of avoiding nothingness and how it serves impressive decisiveness in further venture creation. The "avoidingness" of-not-being-all-that-one-can is again present in the following vignette:

> One of the differences between anxiety and fear in Heidegger's philosophy is that fear is about something tangible, whereas anxiety is a mood or condition about something more indistinct.
>
> > Yep it's stressful, because in the back of my head you know I've always worked right from as a teenager, so my parents have always encouraged me to work hard and so it sounds great to be able to say, look mum can I have 50 thousand dollars or whatever the amount is, then they give it to you. It's not in my personality or it's not the way they taught me to just take money off people.
>
> This feeling of anguish, of the terrible possibility of not being all that one can is strong enough to drive the entrepreneur. Even though they were not brought up to accept money from others, even though

> there was a genuine concern about accepting money from his parents
> who were not wealthy, the possibility of Nothingness (Åsvoll 2012) is
> revealed through the fact that he still accepted the funds.
>
> Hancock (2013, p. 163)

It is not only the experience of Angst and nothing that motivates, but
also the possibility of not-being-at-home anymore. The next vignette
shows that the alternative of nothing is not a preferred way of being-
in-the-(entrepreneurial)-world.

Time is fundamental, and death, while not necessarily in the front of
one's mind, is a constant reminder of our mortality and the temporality of nothing in the context of being in the world, dasein. As one
participant recounted regarding her parents in-law:

> I think their theory is going to be, Look we're going to be dead
> in 20 years we can't take it with us. We've got the money; we're
> doing it, if we didn't have the money, we'd have just told you.

These entrepreneurs and their family financiers certainly feel the need
to be in the world, to be in a decision-making paradigm that takes
control and moves toward a life that could be, rather than the alternative of nothing.

Hancock (2013, p. 166).

Moreover, the importance of funding as a form of (avoiding) nothingness
seems to constitute a platform to become entrepreneurial. For these entrepreneurs (musicians and family entrepreneurs), the life-project is in different ways dependent upon a sort of nothingness practice. More vignettes are
given in order to show how nothing might appear in a variety of ways:

Vignette

As mentioned earlier, in Rennemo and Åsvoll (2016), four entrepreneurs
were given a more socio-material task. Here each of the entrepreneurs is
asked to pick a picture as a tool for reflection from a stack of cards contain-
ing one hundred pictures. When choosing a card, we asked the entrepreneurs
to look for one that speaks to them and tells them something about their

business five years from now. After picking the picture, they all were asked to tell their story related to the picture. Below, some empirical findings are presented in terms of a perspective of nothing.

Deborah picked two pictures and tells something about both.

Figure 4.1 Heavy burden

Figure 4.2 Tree of security

In this sequence, Deborah tells: I feel like this now. The picture illustrates that I'm bearing a heavy burden. Now I feel exactly like this,
but I do not want the situation to continue. Within five years, I hope
there are only five books to carry. Now, I do not feel my head above
the water. The tree symbolizes growth, both in terms of disciplinarity,
required staffing, economics and with regard to necessary equipment—
it grows. With regard to myself, green is also a very stress reducing
colour. I think I need this tranquillity, the grounding and anchoring
that a tree offers. It symbolizes security regarding the decisions you
have to make and also that it is here you want to be. There is a lot of
energy in everything green and everything growing and then I think;
this is what I want.

This vignette reveals that angst is the feeling that arises when there is an
"impossibility of projecting oneself upon a potentiality-for-being which
belongs to existence and which is founded primarily upon one's objects of
concern" (Heidegger 1962, p. 393). The nothing feeling of "*I do not want
the situation to continue*" emerges in the next vignette.

Figure 4.3 Not at home

As we can see, she is talking to the picture, and the other three women entrepreneurs are listening to her, looking at her, confirming her story.

Then it was Cathrin's turn. She chose a picture illustrating a mountain climber.

> The first thing I thought about when I saw this mountain climber was about my own situation in five years. When I look at the picture, I think that if the right buyer appears, then maybe I will sell my company. I also think, all the time, it is not far to the top of the mountain. This is a mountain climber, I myself [am] dealing with diving in my spare time. Within five years, I hope to spend some more time doing recreational activities.

As seen in the situational picture, when this entrepreneur wearing a blue T-shirt speaks, she is looking at the picture, maybe in fact realizing the presence of nothing or that she is perhaps not-at-home anymore and nothing is more present. Being-in-the-world, she-and-the-picture dwell in something new, and it may be "here and now" projecting new places and existential possibilities in the future. This "mountain climber picture" is reflecting Nothing possibilities, and the possibility being someone else or of not being a (full-time) entrepreneur any longer (i.e. more time doing recreational activities).

It is easy to ignore the fact that nothing (i.e. the no-thing that is being itself) supports the entrepreneurial practical (pre)understanding of being, that entrepreneurial practices are the "groundless ground" of our being-in-the-world. But this fact "emerges" in the experience of Angst, which is not just an ontic, psychological state, but one that has genuine ontological, existential importance.

Summary

The events that take place form an entrepreneurial life and venture creations where the events are tied into everyday life. They are not just facing uncertainty as a lack of information, but they face a kind of radical uncertainty that questions their identity and challenges their life-projects such as becoming entrepreneurs. The character of these "powerless", "restless" and "survival" events can be interpreted as nothingness, i.e. Angst as the feeling and moment of not-being-at-home in the (entrepreneurial) life-project. Within the decision-making paradigm, unexpected existential moments and consequences and incalculable results are created. Angst/not-being-at-home experiences cannot be considered as mere side effects of decision-making (see 2.2). In a way, the "side effects" may enlarge the regions of ignorance and not codified knowledge, waiting to be the new source of anxious concerns and existential nothingness. The decision-making and applicable paradigm may generate more unknowns outside the immediate reach of the "enframed" concern. Therefore a perspective based on the notion of decision-making as a mutual concern for being and nothingness has been suggested in order to start to reflect upon the textures which interweave (entrepreneurial) life, nothingness and decision-making (technology) (see 2.1–2.3).

4.3   Projection

The previous themes have highlighted the process whereby entrepreneurs become entrepreneurial by stressing the importance of applicable paradigm/ technology and Angst/nothing. Here, the focus is sharper on entrepreneurs' future perspectives and their self-understanding when faced with an open horizon of possibilities. This section aims at showing how beings project being "thrown into" the future, that is to say, how the future is important in the process of becoming entrepreneurial, and how entrepreneurs evaluate themselves and their options to move forward in time and to be "timely".

Hauge (2011) grasps the two musicians Jan Kenneth and Knut Magne's focus on ongoing projects that are in the process of future recognition and actualization in order to make sense: She comments:

> When Jan Kenneth and Knut Magne move into new projects, they act on behalf of their hermeneutic lived experiences. Lived experience is utilized to make more informed guesses about what kind of actualities will help move their artistic and entrepreneurial ambitions and identity further into a completeness in order to redesign identity, meaning and make sense, even though the process is not to be finalized. (Hauge 2011, p. 139). . . . Musicians can never be sure that their artwork and business ideas will result in symbols characterized as entrepreneurial successes. The process of becoming entrepreneurial and at the same time redesigning artistic creativity is a complex, authentic and evaluative process. The process starts "at home" using the tools and resources available. Ergo; becoming is a never-ending story where beings are "thrown into" the future as their past experiences serve as guidelines for how to cope in-the-world to get a best possible outcome of life.
>
> (Hauge 2011, p. 120)

I infer from this passage that it is possible to make sense and to appreciate acting on what's always already there (hermeneutical lived experiences) in the (projecting) process of becoming entrepreneurial. More specifically, it is possible to project how this "thrown into" the future might look, i.e. the musicians' relation to tools are important with regard to being entrepreneurial. Hauge (2011, p. 123) writes:

Vignette

> I had a few loudspeaker elements that would be perfect for building a sub [a big bass]. I told Rune about the size of the elements and asked him how big the loudspeaker box would have to be if the loudspeaker was built on the horn principle. My question to Rune was how can you get the maximum effect out of a given driver, if you do not think about box limits?

Rune found Knut Magne's challenge exciting. He spent three days simulating the bass horn and sketching a design that he sent back to Knut Magne, who immediately after receiving the design started to build the sub. The design follows the same principle as the ancient Roman amphitheatres. The speaker is placed in the narrow bottom of a funnel where he/she speaks in the direction of the wide funnel top. When people speak on such stages, their voices can reach thousands of people. The seven-metre sub was placed under the Mill stage floor, and it worked perfectly. After impressing his Bachelor examiners, Rune kept on working on his sub solution, using the Mill stage as a reference test station. This enabled him to get a foothold in the very small Norwegian loudspeaker-building milieu and to establish Paragon Arrays AS.

This vignette is just a snapshot of a continuing and open-ended process for those two musicians who later became world famous in the (extreme) metal music world and business. Nevertheless, what is portrayed here is how the development of a new tool (extreme sub) not only leads to a new venture creation (Paragon Arrays AS), but actualizes new potentials and possibilities in the musicians' life-projects and the world music of sound. This vignette shows how projection might work, that is to say, how understanding of penetrates into possibilities (Heidegger 1962).

Summary

In line with what this technology and applicable paradigm (Heideggerian-influenced) section suggests, researchers like Hjorth and Steyaert (2004) and Sarasvathy (2001) also support the importance of equipment (although in different ways).

Or more specifically, they also attest to is the fact that a main feature of entrepreneurial life is not just a presence of equipment, but a questioning relationship with equipment. As shown in the example of creating the new sub amplifier, the entrepreneur is able to upgrade and replace tools in ways that upset established uses or suggest new ones (for more literature see Berglund 2007; Cope 2005; Hjorth, Jones, and Gartner 2008).

To recall the previous examples of entrepreneurs' relationships to tools such as money, funding, business plans, marketing strategies etc., it may seem that these tools indeed are a means to an end or something that can be exchanged. However, vignettes also show how entrepreneurs can disrupt the applicable ready-to-hand technology, finding possibilities and opportunities in encouraging others to rethink what is typically concealed in their equipmentality. How, then to proceed? Maybe it is possible to research and look beyond equipmentality by considering whether entrepreneurs might experience moments of undecidedness and pre-decision in which the objects of being in business become lost. In this perspective, we find in the phenomenology of living expressions of what Heidegger calls "nothing" a persistent lingering with things marked by thoughts that do not succumb to the restlessness of applicable paradigm or what academics might conceptualize as a proto-entrepreneurial figure. An altogether different sense of interest emerges, demanding that we suspend our concern for things as means for our projects awhile and simply project and dwell with them.

Remarks on Vignettes and Examples

It seems tentatively that there is a link between the idea of technology/applicable paradigm to the meaning of entrepreneurship and nothingness (not-being-at-home), projections, in the lives of the entrepreneurs. But first, can we be sure that the phenomenon of Nothing and Angst exists at all in entrepreneurial practice? If not, the theory of Nothing may be considered as just metaphysical speculation without empirical relevance and trustworthiness.

After conducting a large number (sixteen) of interviews, followed by a phenomenological reduction, Hancock (2013, pp. 165–166) concludes that:

> The Angst of nothingness, of "falling" or "slipping away" from the world to an inauthentic existence and not feeling "at home" with oneself is clearly evident from these participants. These entrepreneurs' heightened sense of nothing appears to provide the spark, the drive, and the ability to overcome fear to follow their passion. . . . This study strongly suggests that entrepreneurs may feel a heightened sense of nothingness. A clear motivation for taking on present day fear (risk) in order to alleviate the dread of not achieving all that is possible in being.

One implication might be as follows; this downward plunge into and within the groundlessness of the technological Being of the "applicable" has a kind of motion which constantly tears the understanding away from the projecting of nothing possibilities, and into the tranquillized supposition that it possesses everything within its reach. Since the understanding is thus constantly torn away from nothing and into the "applicable" (though always with a potential crack of nothing), the movement of nothing may be characterized *in different ways*. So, then, is it possible to see patterns in nothing experiences? Examples and vignettes suggest that entrepreneurs are involved in different "nothing" experiences, i.e. from their life as the avoidance behaviour (keeping nothing away) to the severe loss of the taken-for-granted way of being-in-the-world. Based on this material, I will describe three ways in which entrepreneurs may "suffer" and take advantage of the nothing experience:

> **Being slow** involves the entrepreneur slowing down activity (i.e. marketing, funding, business plans) until it becomes halting and there is a potential for a remote uncanniness (and perhaps passivity becomes more dominant; cf. chapter 2.3).
>
> **Being lost (into threshold)** is about the entrepreneur's difficulty finding her way in an unfamiliar world, being lost in the world of places, of equipment, and of activity. However, every "lost" act or nothing moment exhibits potentiality for what may come.
>
> **Being a blank** is about being in an empty world wherein entrepreneurs are unable to find the thoughts and words that make it possible for them to engage in a reflective act. The significance of experience is temporarily lost and the entrepreneur is not-at-home anymore. This is also the greatest potential for re-inventing the self-understanding and being grasped by possibilities and projections for new life-projects. (Passivity is an all-encompassing feature; cf. chapter 2.3).

The stability of technology apparently keeps nothing away. Apparently, because when technology and the always already applicable fails (i.e. financial analysis did not predict sudden bankruptcy), business failure or unexpected events make entrepreneurial practice almost impossible, existential nothing appears. Nothing experiences as in the most crude forms reveal the feeling of not-being-at-home anymore (uncanniness). The promise of technology and dwelling places is not first and foremost profit or prosperous entrepreneurial business life, but the false assumption of scrutiny and keeping nothing away. This all-encompassing basis for the applicable paradigm, which tool-based technology rests on, nevertheless becomes aware of themselves (as this chapter may have shown).

Notes

1. The main motivation behind Hancock's (2013) dissertation is to investigate why people engage in within-family finance in order to start a new enterprise. The thesis is investigated through the philosophical lens of phenomenology. Sixteen people who either provided or received funds within a family relationship were interviewed. The findings consist of three (Heideggerian) themes named care, Angst and tenacity. One of the aims is to connect lived experiences from the participant with theory grounded in phenomenological philosophy

2. "The objective of this thesis is to describe the process by which musicians become entrepreneurial. In this dissertation, becoming entrepreneurial mean that musicians undertake commercial activities that are necessary for artistic creativity and performance. In order to analyse the entrepreneurial process, I have investigated a group of metal musicians, for whom acting entrepreneurially is a life strategy as a musician in a changing world. Making money is rarely metal musicians' motivation in entrepreneurial processes; instead their "inspiration is the musicians' independent creative desire that contributes to their self-realization" (Hauge 2011, p. 7). . . . "Having investigated 'my' three musicians and retold their stories about their ambitions and objectives in living the metal musical life, I come to a few conclusions about how musicians become entrepreneurial. The fourth chapter discusses the thesis' conclusions, starting by arguing that how extreme metal musicians become entrepreneurs is about having a life project, which Heidegger might have referred to as 'setting up a world' constituted by the musicians' artworks. The process of musicians becoming entrepreneurial is thus a result of beings' existence and engagement in a complex world on the move, where becoming entrepreneurial is a process of designing and redesigning a lifestyle" (Hauge 2011, p. 8).

3. This data open up several theoretical interpretations which are not pursued in the forthcoming article (Rennemo and Åsvoll 2016). In the article, we suggest that the notions of (Bakhtinian) borderline dialogues and places to (be)come act as central drivers and conditions for meaning around which diverse entrepreneurs coalesce. Especially interesting, and a future line of inquiry, is perhaps the resemblance or parallel between the Bakhtinian dialogue and surplus of vision and (different modes of) nothing. For more see Rennemo and Åsvoll (2018). However, focusing on four entrepreneurs in "in situ" dialogues and places to become in entrepreneurial practice, the article examines how entrepreneurs' existence and learning unfold from their dialogues in Ba. All of them participated in a four-and-a-half hour meeting, with a thirty-minute lunch break. The day of data collection was designed by the two researchers. The whole meeting was recorded with a double set of cameras, providing optimal opportunities to observe the participants' communication and body language.

References

Åsvoll, H. (2012). On Heidegger, "Theory of Nothing" and entrepreneurship: A prologue to an entrepreneurial philosophy of nothing. *Academy of Entrepreneurship Journal*, 18(1), 55–75.

Berglund, H. (2007). Opportunities as existing and created: A study of entrepreneurs in the Swedish mobile internet industry. *Journal of Enterprising Culture*, 15(3), 243–273.

Cope, J. (2005). Toward a dynamic learning perspective of entrepreneurship. *Entrepreneurship Theory and Practice*, 29(4), 373–397.

Hancock, G. (2013). *For love or money: Understanding the dynamics of within-family finance for a start-up enterprise: A phenomenological investigation*. Ph.D. dissertation. University of Adelaide, Australia.

Hauge, E. (2011). *How do metal musicians become entrepreneurial? A phenomenological investigation on opportunity recognition*. Ph.D. dissertation. Norwegian Business School, Norway.

Heidegger, M. (1927/1962). *Being and Time*. New York: Harper & Row Publishers.

Hjorth, D., Jones, C. & Gartner, W. (2008). Introduction to recreating/recontextualising entrepreneurship. *Scandinavian Journal of Management*, 24(2), 81–84.

Hjorth, D. & Steyaert, C. (2004). *Narrative and Discursive Approaches in Entrepreneurship: A Second Movement in Entrepreneurship Book*. Cheltenham: Edward Elgar Publishing.

Popp, A. & Holt, R. (2013). The presence of entrepreneurial opportunity. *Business History*, 55(1), 9–28.

Rennemo, Ø. & Åsvoll, H. (2016). *Dialogues and places to be(come) in entrepreneurial BA practice*. Proceedings 8th International Process Symposium, Corfu, Greece.

Sarasvathy, S. D. (2001). Causation and effectuation: Toward a theoretical shift from economic inevitability to entrepreneurial contingency. *The Academy of Management Review*, 26(2), 243–264.

Spinoza, C., Flores, F. & Dreyfus, H. (1997). *Disclosing New Worlds: Democratic Action and the Cultivation of Solidarity*. Cambridge: MIT Press.

Young, J. (2000). What is dwelling? The homelessness of modernity and the worlding of the world. In M. Wrathall & J. Malpass (eds.), *Heidegger, Authenticity and Modernity*. Cambridge: MIT Press. 187–204.

5 Outlining a Model of Nothing Modes

I propose a four-fold model with nominal curves to show the importance and potential of "Nothing" within entrepreneurship. The model includes modes such as surfacing "Nothing", embedding "Nothing", sharing "Nothing", and inducing "Nothing" resonance (see Figure 5.1). This model implies a move from the ontological framework to an epistemological perspective; that is to say, more focus is placed on how knowledge unfolds than on how existence moves forward. Before the different modes in the model are shown, I will explain how the model was created.

This model is created by theoretical speculation including the simple underlying features or logic of knowledge management. Roughly speaking, knowledge management can be said to consist of three main components, namely knowledge acquisition, performance and distribution. I have attempted to transfer these three components to an understanding of nothing in various modes. In this respect, there are no pat answers as to how the various nothing modes can be understood based on the three main components in knowledge management. To repeat, this is a theoretical speculation as part of an attempt at showing how nothing may perform in different arenas and in different ways. My rationale and theory-inspired exercise is as follows: different ways of acquiring nothing can be shown via surfacing and embedding; both distribution and performance can be visualized with the aid of resonance and sharing.

5.1 Surfacing Nothing

The first approach toward letting "Nothing" reveal itself is surfacing "Nothing". As entrepreneurs practise and experience throughout life, they generate a significant amount of information, knowledge and emotions that become embodied and work as a part of their unconscious mind and way of being and nothing. Even though an entrepreneur may have difficulty retrieving it when needed, to let their being and unconsciousness reveal themselves

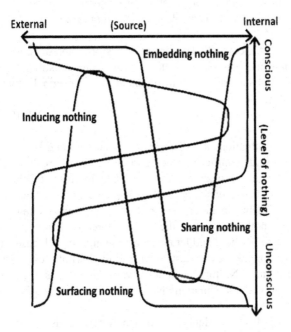

Figure 5.1 Model of Nothing Modes

can become a valuable source in entrepreneurial life. Surfacing "Nothing" is focused on allowing the "benefit" of that which is "Nothing" from the unconscious to conscious nothing. Here, I propose that there are two ways by which "Nothing" can be surfaced: through external triggering and internal dialogue.

Triggering

As represented in Figure 5.1, the process of triggering is primarily externally driven engaging internal participation and dwelling.

For example, an (external) situation, conversation, questions with specific conditions may trigger the surfacing of "Nothing" available to respond. The unconscious is aware of the flow of consciousness, available to affect decisions as the situation is associated with internal information/"Nothing". In these cases, the "Nothing" surfaced from the unconscious may be described as implicit, with externally generated situation mixing with "Nothing" in order to create that surfaced implicit "Nothing". Triggering may be the phenomenon that occurs in a (external) situation, where an immediate decision must be made that could have significant consequences. The term Situation is pivotal, for *situation* is not something we enter into, nor does it exist independent of inquiry. Here is the detailed listening to Dewey:

> Inquiry is the controlled or directed transformation of an indeterminate situation into one that is so determinate in its constituent distinctions and relations as to convert the elements of the original situation into a unified whole.
>
> (Dewey 1938/1991, p. 108)

Indeterminate situations are those in which an entrepreneur may dwell in nothing, and finds conflict between current needs and realities. The indeterminacy can range from feeling foreign to implicit stakeholder goals, hidden assumptions, unshared collegial expectations, which may result in severe problems in entrepreneurial practice. That feeling of indeterminacy and "nothing" is then the driving force of inquiry, enabling the entrepreneur to be-there and let nothing show up. In such cases, the entrepreneur as inquirer seeks to establish a unified whole, one that replaces the indeterminacy/"Nothing" with a unity. In other words, the entrepreneur changes a problematic situation/"Nothing" and is changed in (being) turn through actions.

This also indicates a double tension between conditions of existence, that is to say, between nothing and being (or through the essential struggle between earth and world as also Heidegger would have said). What Heidegger (1962) himself suggests is not just that the "nothing" emerges from the ordinary (i.e. that the nothing makes itself visible in Van Gogh's painting of an ordinary pair of shoes) but also the reverse, that what we now think of as "ordinary" first originated out of the "nothing". For Heidegger (1962) extraordinary creations (i.e. radical innovations), once brought into being (by entrepreneurs), eventually become stabilized in intelligibility and so perceived as merely "ordinary" (in much the same way that what begins as a revealing insight is eventually routinized. Being and nothing within entrepreneurial context may change or transform each other. Maybe this insight can be explored further by drawing on the philosophy of John Dewey.

Dewey (1974) points out that it is within this very interplay or interaction between the entrepreneur and the environment that experience commences, and it is primarily relational and social in nature from an evolutionary perspective. Based on the interaction principle, it is equally interesting to focus on temporal aspects and a continuity that is able to provide the experience of "Nothing" with the necessary quality. The continuity of experience is a principle which holds that "every experience enacted and undergone modifies the one who acts and undergoes, while this modification affects, whether we wish it or not, the quality of subsequent experiences" (Dewey 1974, p. 47).

This statement underscores the past and the future as two important dimensions of the construction of experience.

We may construct a new experience out of nothing, that is to say, out of a reliance on the experiences of the past. We can also see this insight in a refined question found in Plato's Meno dialogue: How can you know that it was what you did not know? The question is worded as a logical paradox and is well suited to confuse and seduce. It is confusing if one thinks "what I know, I know; what I do not know, I do not know", and these two insights cannot be consistent or otherwise correlate with one another. This is the language of logic that Dewey (1974) wants to transcend. The point is that you cannot know anything new and create new experiences if it is possible to link it with some precedent, an experience from the past activated and transformed in a present situation. Hence, the factual basis we have available in a specific "Nothing"/problem situation is not adequate for creating an experience; it is also necessary to benefit from previous experiences. These are woven together with contemporary problems that are solved in a future perspective. Thinking and reflection may help one to escape from daily, routine-like education. An entrepreneur who reflects, for example, over how feedback from the market can be interpreted finds himself in a vacuum. This vacuum results in the entrepreneur directing his action towards the future and future market situations which are conducive to new feedbacks. In contrast to an entrepreneur who is merely caught up in routines and is thereby steered from behind (by the past), the entrepreneur who reflects in the absence of routines is steered from the front (by the future). It is a matter only of allowing present or immediate experiences to play a "prank" on the teacher and to create a doubt that can be fruitful in the future. Dewey (1974, p. 41) emphasizes this continuity:

> Hence the central problem of an education based upon experience is to select the kind of present experiences that live fruitfully and creatively in subsequent experiences.

The key notion here is that the past, the present and the future are interwoven. "Nothing" can be an experience that preserves the present moment, which later can yield better practical results and solve problems. Such a process embodies and requires an element of uncertainty and doubt. Both Dewey (1974) and Peirce (1960) stress this kind of (problematic) doubt contingent on external (trigger) factors.

For Peirce (1960), doubt arises from surprise or as he says:

> genuine doubt always has an external origin, usually from surprise; and that it is as impossible for a man to create in himself a genuine doubt

by such an act of the will as would suffice to imagine the condition of a mathematical theorem, as it would be for him to give himself a genuine surprise by a simple act of the will.

(Para. 5, p. 443)

Thus it is possible to understand "Nothing" as resting on external triggering, in terms of an everyday sense-making (being), indeterminate Situation (Dewey) and abduction (Peirce).

Internal Dialogue

Although dialogue is generally thought about as communication or interactions among individuals within an entrepreneurial context, there is another dialogue that is less understood. This is the process of entrepreneurs consciously "dialogizing" with themselves. What this means is the conscious mind learning to communicate with, listen to, and dwell in its own unconscious and "Nothing". One way to dialogizing and listen within yourself is through creating an internal dialogue (Bakhtin 1993). For example, accepting the authenticity of and listening deeply to a continuous stream of conscious thought while following the tenets of dialogue. Those tenets would include: withholding quick judgement, not demanding quick answers, and exploring underlying assumptions, then looking for *meaning between what the entrepreneur consciously thinks and what she feels*. Bakhtin outlines such an approach as dialogical relationship or in other words:

> it offers us the possibility that, in our very utterance of words to ourselves in our own inner speech, we can also think not only dialogically, but also polyphonically in terms of many different "voices" with different "logical" points of view, and also with our different inner expressions being related to each other with many different affective or emotional-volitional tones.

(Shotter 2008, p. 17)

Different meanings, thoughts and opinions are instead reflected and indwelled—the multiple "voices" being encouraged and tolerated. None of the voices are taken-for-granted or as having the priority amongst different constructions. When it comes to the process of an internal dialogue, it requires listening to voices engaged in the dialogue to admit the possibility of change and re-construction of one's views and perspectives. Therefore, the possible change and transformation within oneself (the entrepreneur) may serve as a criterion of a dialogic interaction based on "Nothing"/the not-being-at-home experience. However, internal dialogues are not easy to arouse.

Perhaps entrepreneurs too often tend to oppose a true dialogue, because they are often reluctant to change or feel uncomfortable (with "Nothing") within the entrepreneurial context. Accordingly, entrepreneurs block their capacity for exploring new possibilities and ideas because they become complacent, remain rigid and refuse to admit the possibility of change.

However, in order to fully embrace the potential of this (dialogical) dwelling, it may be necessary for entrepreneurs to first recognize where their experiences of "Nothing" are coming from. Recall (from Dewey and the continuity principle) that "Nothing" may surface from continuous mixing of (external) situation with internal information/"Nothing". This means that when the entrepreneur dwells and listens to unconsciousness, he/she is listening to the semantic web or complexing of the experiences, learning, thoughts and feelings throughout life. Thus the process of dialogue (dialogizing "Nothing") in the unconscious is related to lifelong conscious learning experiences (more on this issue in the section below on embedding "Nothing").

5.2 Embedding Nothing

The second approach towards letting "Nothing" be is embedding. Here, "Nothing" is not a private (potential) kind of intelligibility cut off from the everyday. Intelligibility is the result of the gradual refinement of responses that grows out of long experience acting within the shared cultural practices. In figure 5.1 we see that embedding is both externally and internally driven, with "Nothing" moving from the conscious to the unconscious. Embedding "Nothing" in the unconscious can occur through exposure or immersion, by accident or by choice. Examples would include travel, regularly attending business meetings, analyzing recent (market, financial) trends, listening to co-workers and imitating what you have heard in the lunch every day. Further, embedding "Nothing" may occur quietly as an entrepreneur lives through diverse experiences and becomes more proficient at some activity (such as public speaking, pitching visualizing future markets trends etc.).

To shed light on what embedding nothing might be, it is possible to draw on neuroscience. In the late 1990s, neuroscience research identified what are referred to as mirror neurons. As Dobbs (2006, p. 22) explains:

> These neurons are scattered throughout key parts of the brain—the premotor cortex and centers for language, empathy and pain—and fire not only as we perform a certain action, but also when we watch someone else perform that action.

For example, watching a video (see example below) is a form of mimicry that transfers actions, behaviours, norms etc. Thus when we see something being enacted, our mind creates the same patterns that we would use to enact that "something" ourselves (Dobbs 2006). As these patterns fade into long-term memory, they could represent a potential for nothing. While mirror neurons are a subject of current research, I would speculate that they represent a mechanism for the transfer a potential of nothing between entrepreneurs or throughout an entrepreneurial culture. (For more on mirror neurons, see Gazzaniga (2004).

A thought experiment of this would be when an entrepreneurship student is training to become a good business plan pitcher (to present in front of audience crucial factors in a business plan within a short period of time). In doing so she reviews a video of herself successfully pitching to increase her pitching capability. This is a result of the fact that when the entrepreneur performs her perfect pitching, the patterns going through her brain while she is doing it are the same patterns that go through her brain when she is watching herself do it. When she is watching the video she is repeating the desired brain patterns and this repetition strengthens these patterns in unconscious memory. When "doing" the pitching, she cannot think about her actions, nor try to control them. Doing so would degrade her performance because her conscious thoughts would interfere with her performance.

Practice moves beyond exposure to include repeated participation in some skill or process, thus strengthening the patterns in the entrepreneurial mind. As their scope of experience widens, the number of relevant neuronal patterns increases (Dobbs 2006). As an entrepreneurship student becomes more proficient in a specific area through effortful practice, the number of neurons needed to perform the task decreases and the remaining pattern gradually becomes embedded in the unconscious, ergo it (in my view) becomes a potential of concealed "Nothing". When this happens, the reasons and context within which the "Nothing" was "created" often become hidden from consciousness and concealed from being (Dasein).

5.3   Sharing Nothing

The third approach towards building extraordinary consciousness is sharing nothing. In the discussion above on surfacing nothing, it is indicated that surfaced nothing is a kind of new nothing (hence nothing noths or transcends itself), a different shading of that which was in the unconscious. If nothing can be described in words and visuals then this would be by definition explicit. Yet the subject of this paragraph is sharing nothing. The key is that it is not necessary to make nothing explicit in order to share it.

Then, with regard to the figure, sharing nothing occurs both consciously and unconsciously, although nothing shared remains concealed in nature. In my perspective the power of this process has been recognized in organizations for years, and tapped into through the use of mentoring and shadowing programmes to facilitate imitation and mimicry. More recently, it has become the focus of group learning, where communities and teams engage in dialogue focused on specific issues and develop a common frame of reference, perhaps intersubjectivity and understanding that can create solutions to complex problems. These solutions may retain "concealed" in terms of understanding the complexity of the issues (where it is impossible to identify all the contributing factors much less a cause and effect relationship among them). Hence, these solutions would not be explainable in words and visuals to entrepreneurs outside the team or community. When this occurs, the team (having arrived at the "concealed" decision) will often create a rational explanation of why the decision makes sense to communicate to outside stakeholders, partners, clients etc.

To understand sharing nothing more in detail I offer a thought example on mentoring: assume that a mentor in higher entrepreneurship education assumed the role of "virtual" CEO, taking on many of the top-level executive functions of the new company, while the student observes and learns. After a while the student noted that his mentor, who came into the company as acting president, demonstrated how to effectively build the team, establish priorities, manage disputes etc. This may be a kind of modelling of behaviour for a student where learning and being, and hence the potential of nothing takes place informally and often unconsciously. When looking at this thought example it is tempting to draw on Heidegger's *dwelling place, which* emphasizes how the entrepreneurship student and mentor feel "at home" in this context of sharing (nothing). The student learns by his engagement in a given dwelling place how to get on within that social context. Both mentor and student actions, which make up that *getting on*, shape their being and potential nothing, collectively, the potential for nothing to show itself.

5.4   Inducing Nothing

The fourth approach toward sensitizing "Nothing" is inducing resonance. Through exposure to provocative and opposing ideas (them and us, I-Other), terms and perspectives that have a potential for indwelling and aroused commitment, it is possible to create a resonance within the receiver or entrepreneur that amplifies the meaning of the incoming information, increasing its emotional content and receptivity. In Figure 5.1, to bring into conscious awareness. inducing resonance may happen when external stimuli resonating with *internal* information/"Nothing" When resonance occurs, the stimuli or incoming information is consistent with *the outer borders of "Nothing"*, i.e. what may be manifested as a frame of reference and belief systems within the receiving entrepreneur.

In other words, situated in the feeling of not-being-at-home in this world (not yet being found by the relevant commitment, not being discovered by a direction and life-project), inducing resonance may lead innovators and entrepreneurs in another direction or to start another (life-) project. An example of inducing resonance may be illustrated by some quotes from Steve Jobs working with the Mac project: "It's more fun to be a pirate than to join the Navy" (Sculley and Byrne 1988, p. 157). "Innovation has nothing to do with how many R&D dollars you have. When Apple came up with the Mac, IBM was spending at least 100 times more on R&D. It's not about money. It's about the people you have, how you're led, and how much you get it" (Kirkpatrick 1998).

As a brief sum up; the role of Jobs as product champion was critical, but he also introduced major complications into the development process. Moritz (1984, p. 129) observed that:

> Some at Apple thought the entire Mac project reflected a parade of personal idiosyncrasies rather than any grand design. There was no plan of Napoleonic proportions. False starts, diversions, mistakes, experiments, rebellion, and competition formed the stuff of the machine.

Maybe the lack of support from the top management was compensated by Jobs's commitment and articulated vision of "Nothing". He was determined to build a computer that was in his words "insanely great". A crucial element in his "transferred nothing" is the involvement of personal (existence) commitment and the understanding of emotional beings/nothings. This is about how drive and commitment to push the idea forward are handled and how it is distributed (by transferring nothing) in the Mac team. Maybe the purpose of a Jobs's inducing resonance is to transfer "Nothing" and play on how external information is communicated and at best tied to emotional tags (explicitly expressed as Pirate):

> Steve Jobs has always understood that, as human beings, our first relationship with anything is an emotional one. . . . A device isn't just a sum of its functions; it's something that should make you smile, you should cradle, you should love, you should have an emotional relationship with. If people think that's pretentious, then, in a sense, the success of Apple proves how wrong they are.
> (www.treehugger.com/culture/steve-jobs-understood-something-about-emotions-that-the-green-movement-too-often-ignores.html)

The aesthetics of this (emotional) process is that this occurs on both sides of a question such that the active listener (i.e. in the Mac team) who has an interest in the innovation project is pulled into one side or another (choosing between "boring" navy like Microsoft or pirate radical Apple). An eloquent speaker such as S. Jobs perhaps tried to speak from the audience's (Mac Team) frame of reference to tap into their "Nothing" or feeling of not yet being-at-home, but with the promises and vision of a different pirate being/ existence. Perhaps he sometimes at best came across as confident, likable and positive to transfer "Nothing", and may well refer to higher order purpose, i.e., to connect with the listener's/Mac team commitment to change themselves (not perceiving itself as mere Microsoft technicians, but as a pirate/unpredictable innovators) and the world by new products (inventing a user-friendly PC).

This resonance of "Nothing" amplifies feelings connected to the incoming information while also validating the re-creation of skills and commitment in the receiver. Further, this process results in the amplification and transformation of "Nothing" from tacit to implicit (or explicit). Since "Nothing" as being is now accessible at the conscious level, this process also may create a sense of ownership within the listener. The speakers are not telling the listener what to believe; rather, when the "Nothing" of the receiver resonates with what the speaker is saying (and how it is said), an expansion of understanding occurs within the listener based upon a tacit relation (*mitdasein*). This may actualize the potential of relational "Nothing" and being-in-the-world.

Summary and Remarks

One eminent challenge is that it can be difficult to take deliberate and planned advantage of important "Nothing" aspects and possibilities (cf. four-fold nothing model) of entrepreneurs. This is due to the nature of "Nothing"; "It is always ready, though it only seldom springs, and we are snatched away and left hanging" (Heidegger 1993, p. 93). This "always already" (hermeneutical language) may be called a form of predictable unpredictability, which does give much chance for other than nothing phenomena emerging unexpectedly. From Polanyi (1967, p. 4) it's stated that entrepreneurs know more that they can ever tell and I may add, more than they can do. Or more radically, first and foremost "Nothing" provides possibilities of existential character, possibilities which perhaps never becomes fully conscious or acted upon, possibilities which never show up as learning outcomes and entrepreneurial products. For example, implicit stakeholder goals, hidden finance assumptions, unshared marked expectations often result in severe problems and "Nothing" possibilities in the entrepreneurial practice.

I present a model that may support entrepreneurs in surfacing, embedding and sharing "Nothing" during their life-projects and entrepreneurial practice. However, this model is not suitable for ready-made solutions or prescribed procedures. In short, you cannot provoke nothing, because nothing comes to you first. You do not control nothing; nothing controls you. You cannot construct or manipulate nothing; nothing constructs you. So when Heidegger (1962) asks rhetorically, "But on what basis does Dasein disclose itself in resoluteness?" he answers:

> Only the resolution itself can give the answer. One would completely misunderstand the phenomenon of resoluteness if one should suppose that this consists simply in taking up possibilities that have been proposed and recommended.

(p. 345)

This is a part of the crucial passive element of nothing (cf. 2.3), which sheds light on how far the term nothing can be stretched. Whether or not the model is compatible with Heideggerian (fundamental) ontological project is an interesting question, because the model "epistemologizes" the terminology originally associated with "Nothing", being and Dasein. However, I do not wish to equivocate the ontological-ontical terminology or treat them as though they were interchangeable. I think it is important to proceed with a clear respect for the line between ontological/ontical and existential/existentiell. While potential conceptual quandaries between the ontological discourse of Heideggerian theory and the ontical discourse of epistemological (Dewey, Bakhtin, Peirce) approaches exist (even though it is not possible to pursue this issue here), Heidegger's fundamental ontology may have profound implications for understanding the relevance of the model, and the (Heideggerian) Nothing may benefit a lot from Bakhtinian, Peircian and Deweyan insights.

References

Bakhtin, M. M. (1993). *Toward a Philosophy of the Act.* (Ed.) V. Liapunov. Austin: Texas University Press.

Dewey, J. (1938/1991). Logic: The theory of inquiry. In J. A. Boydston (ed.), *John Dewey: The Later Works, 1925–1953*, Vol. 12. Carbondale, IL: SIU Press. 1–527 (Originally published in 1938).

Dewey, J. (1974). *The Child and the Curriculum.* Chicago: University of Chicago Press.

Dobbs, D. (2006). A revealing reflection. *Scientific American Mind*, 17(2), 22–27.

Gazzaniga, M. S. (2004). *The Cognitive Neurosciences III.* Cambridge, MA: The MIT Press.

Heidegger, M. (1962). *Being and Time.* New York: Harper & Row Publishers.

Heidegger, M. (1993). Was ist Metaphysik?. In *M. Heidegger, Wegmarken, Gesamtausgabe*. (Trans.) V. Klostermann, English translation as (Heidegger 1993). Frankfurt: Vittorio Klostermann.

Kirkpatrick, D. (1998). The Second Coming of Apple Through a magical fusion of man—Steve Jobs—and company, Apple is becoming itself again: the little anticompany that could. *Fortune*, November 19. Available at: http://archive. fortune.com/magazines/fortune/fortune_archive/1998/11/09/250834/index.htm [accessed September 2018].

Moritz, M. (1984). *The Little Kingdom*. New York: Morrow.

Peirce, C. S. (1960). *Collected Papers*. Cambridge: Harvard University Press.

Polanyi, M. (1967). *The Tacit Dimension*. New York: Anchor Books.

Sculley, J. & Byrne, J. A. (1988). *Odyssey: Pepsi to Apple: A Journey of Adventure, Ideas, and the Future*. New York: Harper & Row Publishers.

Shotter, J. (2008). *Conversational Realities Revisited: Life, Language, Body and World*. Chagrin Falls: Taos Institute.

Part 3

Implications and Reflections on Nothing for Entrepreneurial Theory, Research and Education

This chapter proposes implications of nothing for entrepreneurial theory, research and education. Nothing may invite too many implications, but here I delineate potential consequences for decision-making and "applicable" theory; how research entrepreneurship focuses critically on aspects that otherwise are under-communicated; and how listening and being-in-the-world may work in education. This chapter is based on the three paired assumptions and alternatives presented in chapter 2.

6 Implications

6.1 Implications for Entrepreneurial Theory

How is it possible to ascertain implications of a theory of nothing for entrepreneurial theory? First, we must be reminded that "Nothing" cannot be a theory in the traditional sense. Whereas theorizing decision-making and opportunities harbours its own challenges, developing concepts about nothing and the fact that the entrepreneur is played (out) by nothing is undoubtedly at odds with the very notion of theory. Here theory implies a shift from the priority of actuality to the priority of possibility. I am trying to show that nothing in entrepreneurship represents a phenomenon that often escapes theorizing in entrepreneurial decision-making and opportunities. Theory is not necessarily concerned with the contemplation of existent decisions or objects. Theory involves stepping back from the world, and dwelling upon things seen as merely present in the world. This theoretical stance is looking at things, without looking at them in terms of use, but in terms of possibilities of (non)use.

Implicating "Nothing" to entrepreneurial theory means that technology is essential to Nothing, but does not presume entrepreneurial opportunities and decision-making. The phenomenon of technology as it works ready-to-hand does not leave us with something like a "prison view" of Nothing, an ontic aspect that may serve to round out the innocuous aspects of this entity. Technology may reveal an essential ontological structure of nothing itself. Far from determining its nocturnal side, it constitutes Nothing's days in their everydayness. It follows that the existential-ontological interpretation makes no ontical assertion about the technological and applicable nature of entrepreneurial practice, not because the necessary evidence (correspondence theory of truth, see 2.1) is lacking, but because the premise of this interpretation is prior to any assertion about decision-making and opportunity. Technology is conceived ontologically as a kind of opening or clearing. Ontically, it is not decided whether the entrepreneur is "discovering or creating" and in the opportunity status, nor does she walk in decision-making terrain, or whether she finds herself in an intermediate stage of uncertainty (lack of information) or risk present-at-hand (analyses). Nevertheless, insofar as a paradigm, theory or perspective makes any such assertions, and if it asserts anything about Nothing as Being-in-the-world, it must come back to the existential structures that have been set forth, provided that its assertions are to make a claim to understanding.

The (theoretical) term entrepreneurship has previously been explored by means of the three paired categories: becoming and being, decision-making and dwelling, activity and passivity (chapter 2). The epistemological perspective (a becoming ontology is quickly turned to a becoming epistemology) is characterized based on the becoming subject (i.e. the entrepreneur, teacher and the student), decision-making (mediating knowledge-developing structures) and activity (i.e. cognition). The ontological Being/Nothing is localized in a dwelling mode and consists of a sphere of passivity. Thus, differences in empirical levels of interpretation may be indicated and established, and distinct descriptions have been attached to these. One-sided and varying epistemological and ontological interpretations make the distinct empirical/example levels visible, as well as the distance between these levels. It is possible to see both versions of Nothing-entrepreneurship, where chapter 4, "Vignettes and Examples" relates closely to the ontological aspects of Nothing such as Being, dwelling and passivity, and chapter 5 "a four-fold model" may frame a more epistemologized becoming, decision-making and activity view of entrepreneurship.

The range between two different analytical probes may be understood based on the lack of a coherent paradigm example in entrepreneurial research. What does that mean? Are epistemological and ontological understandings as an expression for inner (paradigmatic) contradictions mutually exclusive and absolutely incomparable? If the answer is clearly "yes", the book might as well end right here. Instead, one might pose the question in a slightly different way: is it possible and desirable to maintain an ontological perspective in epistemologically oriented entrepreneurial research? Or, in other words, do we need an ontological obligation in the interpretation of Nothing in research? There might be a couple of good reasons to answer affirmatively to this question.

It has been shown that one (Nothing) interpretation of Heidegger's (fundamental) ontology is not dominant in an epistemological and empirical manifestation of entrepreneurship. In this case, it does not necessarily imply anything more than that this ontological approach may be seen as less relevant in empirical research. In a larger context, the relationship between ontology and epistemology would appear differently. Being/existence/Nothing may seem to have a good potential within entrepreneurially oriented research, which may lead to the view that Being-Nothing consequently should be utilized as a tool to promote learning and development based on "complete" established forms of knowledge (business plans, syllabus and curricula). By looking at Nothing as only a tool or as a method in a detailed, planned education and learning plan (like the epistemological approach has the tendency to do) in order to achieve a certain result, it is unavoidable that the primary undecidedness/unfinishedness of Nothing is sacrificed, and thus can no longer be described as ontological Nothing. Ontological Nothing, which might be interpreted in the three idealized forms of "slow", and "blank" (see chapter 6.), may contain a kind of anti-empirical approach to how one would develop plans to make Nothing work in the best possible way—or not work in (pedagogical) situations. Especially in education, it may prove vital to have an understanding of the distance to systematic learning of ontological Nothing as a preventive measure against the belief that all learning is a result of planned educational situations. An ontological understanding of Nothing may be part of a critical perspective for both teachers and researchers. This does not necessarily relate only to the risk of Nothing becoming legitimate for an instrumental error, but also for the utilization of predeterminate conditions in research. While it is possible to view the struggle between ideological positions as an expression for an ontological project, Hjorth and Johannisson (2009, p. 28) claim that:

> Bakhtin's and Vygotsky's ideas are fruitfully combined in so-called problem-based learning when the student's day can start with a writing session in which students are asked to explore their learning—to consider themselves as students of learning and not only students of entrepreneurship. This brings them into a double dialogue: between the student-becoming-professional and the student-becoming-learner; and between knowledge more or less instrumental to their future professional role and knowledge about how they learn.

Such an epistemologically oriented dialogical theory, like all theories on learning and education, is said to possess a set of predeterminate premises as to the (pedagogical) relations that are central and meaningful. Predeterminate premises are pronounced in theoretical terms such as "potential zone of development" or mediation, where more competent others and cognitive constructions (Vygotsky 1978) consist prior to the frameworks set into place for (unpredictable) learning. Such pre-set frameworks often bear with them a universalistic tendency that may pose doubts if utilized consistently and one-sidedly by researchers of entrepreneurship in their empirical analyses. Briefly put, the point is that a (constructivist) theoretical framework based on dialogue might make it easier to find dialogues in which something/

Nothing else is going on. In such cases, the spotlight may be focused on the fact that the relation between researchers' theories and empirical data does not necessarily emphasize the same issues. One of the reasons for this might be that theories are normative and a priori, and in some aspects, of a predeterminate nature. In Hjorth and Johannisson's (2009) case, dialogical learning and "entrepreneurial" dialogues are both a normative and analytical entity. A gap might appear between the undecidedness of Being-Nothing (an indeterminate aspect also found in ontological dialogue) and consistent findings in empirical dialogues in dialogical (educational) spaces as the former is not predeterminate. This comparison is perhaps incomparable in a central aspect, considering that epistemological (empirically oriented "activity" research) and Nothing ontological (dialogue) (philosophy or fundamental ontology) are utilized in different scientific traditions. There is a deeper philosophical argument in the incomparableness behind a strict interpretation of the ontological principle of consistently maintaining a distance to instrumental and isolated tool-like utilization of dialogue and Nothing. When dialogue and Nothing is adjusted to interactional utterances that may be mediated, one type of ontological interpretation must be abandoned for an epistemological perspective. However, this does not forcibly imply a disparagement of ontological ideals as a source of critical empirical research. One might "learn" from Nothing and ontological dialogue that it holds out expectations of real unpredictable (learning/ideological) effects, as well as promotes a critical re-evaluating (methodical) attitude to predeterminate theories/models of entrepreneurial (pedagogical) activity. With a reflected meta-methodical overview, an entrepreneurially oriented researcher can explore methodical and analytical insights by exploring (the understanding of) the undecidedness of Nothing and ontological dialogue. Hence, a binding interpretation of Nothing ontology will sometimes be useful and relevant.

Pursuing such a binding interpretation could have implications for how to understand the applicable or decision-making paradigm in entrepreneurial theory (see. 2.1). What follows are two possible consequences that I call the moderate and strong implication.

The Moderate and Strong Implication

The idea is that a paradigm of decision-making or applicable paradigm (priority of actuality) could, as a mutual dependent part, contain a "theory of the Nothingness" of decisions, i.e. one condition of how decisions arise in the first place (priority of possibility). Such a "theory of Nothingness" would obviously go against the notion of entrepreneurial decision-makers as masters of the situation who can solve any problem (as long as it is recognized as a problem). It seems like the existence of entrepreneurs depends on their ability to make decisions all the time about something or someone else. This is a one-sided view, because entrepreneurs, in their nothingness and Angst for their identity, rely on a being-in-the-world, i.e. being with their environment so as to keep their existence restless and open for disclosure. There is always the danger that the entrepreneurs (or how researchers frame entrepreneurs) are playing the game and ignore the fact that the entrepreneurial being is also played with. But maybe a "theory of Nothing" can be founded on the actual practice of decision-making, where the experience of nothing and Dasein play an important part and are being played with.

One further line of inquiry could be what is called a strong implication of "Nothing"; that is to say, to abandon the opportunity fixation. However, if it is possible to claim that nothing precedes entrepreneurial opportunity practice and decision-making, there is perhaps no fixed and predetermined entrepreneurial decision-making habits. The entrepreneurial self (Dasein) is not predetermined, and while the entrepreneurs' past actions might influence the direction of the future, they do not determine it. Instead it may be that the future shapes the way things turn out for entrepreneurs in that the projects that define them extend into the unpredictable and indefinite future, like the end of the horizon which life-projects can neither occupy nor secure (because a new horizon will arise when we reach the one we see). MacDonald (2000, p. 35) notes Heidegger's use of an ancient Greek time metaphor to illustrate this: "like a rower in a boat, a person fixes his or her position by looking backward, while his or her actions move the boat forwards". Deflected by this never-ending and impenetrable horizon, the entrepreneurial life-projects may come back subtly in an uncanny feeling of not-being-at-home in the things with which they are most familiar. That is, we can come to understand that, for the most part, entrepreneurs "are" already acting as if the future must be like the past. Precisely with this recognition, we can see that this way of being need not be so, and then we are open to see new possibilities within the familiar contours of our already-having-been. In short, change-of-life-projects can occur, and habitual ways of acting can be transformed as has been illustrated above.

Maybe the original aspects entrepreneurs are facing are not the decisions about calculation of profits, utility and reduced to the certainty-equivalent of uncertainty and risks, but the exercise of nothing and the realization of ambition, dreams and the "will" to cope with the unknown future (projection). The aspect of nothing is the aspiration for realizing the meaning of Being as the bundle of possibilities and is different from the notion of rationality implied by the maximizing principles of profits and utility. Perhaps entrepreneurship is nourished by nothing, and therefore, nothing should not be under-communicated in entrepreneurial research. Perhaps a merging takes place and like Alice in Wonderland, we find ourselves in a new reality. This submissiveness makes it possible to understand contexts from new perspectives. Other dimensions become visible and expose themselves. This is the opening offered by Dasein and the theory of Nothing. To summarize, this may also have some implications for how it is possible to conduct research or researching entrepreneurship.

6.2   Implications for Entrepreneurial Research

It can be argued that positivist modes of enquiry in entrepreneurship have resulted in the researcher viewing the "entrepreneur's world as something that can be judged from outside using 'hard' concepts" (Perren and Ram 2004, p. 91). This may imply that there is an assumption that entrepreneurial activity is a nexus whereby "entrepreneurs respond to objective information about opportunities that varies over time and place" (Shane 2003, p. 42). This is a two-fold issue; objective information not only *exists*, but it is also the role of the researcher to be objective while gathering it. What does this mean? First, let us take a step back and look at Cartesian dualism.

A theory of nothing may reject the notion that man's (entrepreneurs and researchers) relation to the world is primarily one of subject to object. In an ontological perspective, it is not engaging to approve Descartes's model of man as a self that is conscious of the objects that make up the external world, and doubting one's own ability to know. To exemplify, Heidegger (1962) has a telling illustration of a man hammering a nail. He points out that unless something goes wrong (for example, if the hammer breaks), the hammerer is not aware of his tool as an object at all. He just gets on and dwells with it. Conscious awareness of an object is just not part of the job (but pre-reflective practice, and hence nothing, is).

It is worthwhile to question whether entrepreneurial research, provided it is equipped with more objectivity, reason, theory, knowledge creation and empirical documentation, actually improves entrepreneurial (research) practice. Perhaps the researchers are aboard a Ship of Fools? If one looks to art and the constraints of life, we find battles being fought on the periphery of reason, battles that have real meaning for our lives and that are staged far away from rationality. Based on a Cartesian cogito-ergo-sum experience, it is modern reason that plays the game, in contrast to a (post-modern) "rationality" that is turned upside down and becomes subjected to the game, and that is perhaps even played out. An entrepreneurial Cartesian approaches the world without losing grip (without losing face) and without putting himself at stake, and he therefore misses what slips past him in a world that has something to impart to him. The Cartesian insistence on maintaining a firm grip or presence has perhaps enabled a sort of objectification of the phenomena of opportunity, meaning that a demand has been raised that the phenomena of opportunity must be tangible, able to be grasped and touched and turned into manipulable, predictable and usable experiences and knowledge. This is something like an entrepreneurial Peer Gynt, who thinks that he is always the "master of situations", whereas he is actually the dupe of random events that comprise a "situation" that grabs, seduces and leads him into veiled lies, thefts and illusions about himself. Peer Gynt, like the Cartesians, wants to be master and fabricator of what can be done, experienced and learnt. To put this another way, researchers looking through Cartesian lenses, or who are experiencing a Cartesian hangover, do not wait, because they find that they have waited long enough, to develop and apply a consistent and relevant theoretical perspective. They have a tendency to act as though they are the "masters of situations". From this point, the path is not long, perhaps, to a more than frequent and unannounced drift away from reality in theories/approaches to reality in practice—a Cartesian reality that confuses theory with practice. It must be concluded that this risk is absolutely present when an affinity for a determinative, a priori, theoretical world takes precedence over a complex, continually changing and diversified practice, which can also be denoted as a practice of opportunities and unpredictable potentials.

It may be, in the case of decision-making and applicable paradigm that certain types of problems have occurred in the (research) field that seem to reinforce themselves. This is possibly reflected in a crisis in the basic concepts in decision theory a crisis that has led to the emergence of questions regarding the usefulness and applicability of the theories (March and Simon 1966). One example is the emergence of the notion that (budding) entrepreneurs do not always act in conformity with how a decision-making and applicable paradigm tells us they should act. Maybe this is due to important considerations, aside from rational decision-making, that this paradigm omits and the "theory of Nothing" may disclose.

Perhaps one consideration comes to light when Gadamer (2004) says that the narrowing of perspective that results from concentrating on method is almost imperceptible to the scientist. He is always already oriented toward the methodological correctness of his procedure—but also, conversely, away from reflection. Rather than rejecting a methodologically based investigation, Gadamer wishes to attack its very lack of reflection concerning its pre-determinedness and its criteria. In the postscript to *Truth and Method*, Gadamer (2004) criticizes, among others, the "Social Sciences", claiming that "However uncertain are the factual bases on which rational management of social life might be possible, a will to believe impels the social sciences onward and drives them far beyond their limits" (p. 557).

It all revolves around his assertion that a "confusion that dominates methodology of the sciences is, I think, the degeneration of the concept of practice" (Gadamer 2004, p. 560), and I would add the terms dwelling and being-in-the-world. This insight cannot be reduced to an investigation or methodology within an entrepreneurially oriented science, but it is an attempt at understanding what the conditions are for an entrepreneurial investigation and practice thereof. It is plausible that one instead goes behind a methodological self-consciousness and demonstrates what interweaves it with the experiences of the researcher in a scientific practice. The experiences of a researcher, therefore, are not necessarily part of a one-sided and dichotomous relationship between practice and methodology.

6.3   Implications of Nothing for Entrepreneurial Education

For the past decades, entrepreneurship educators have been attempting to teach entrepreneurship without consensus on what the proper purpose of teaching should be. As a result, there are currently a large number of approaches to teaching entrepreneurship, with varying degrees of effectiveness (Lautenschlager and Haase 2011; Steeter, Kher, and Jacquette 2011; Vetrivel 2011). Here, I would question the applicable and effectiveness paradigms. For example, if the measuring of the effectiveness of entrepreneurship instruction were done based on the number of students who become successful entrepreneurs within five years of graduation, the results would likely be dismal. Many students do not become entrepreneurs until long after they have left the university, and the effect of their university experience on their success is difficult to measure. Others who do start businesses right out of school are probably not more likely to succeed than someone who did not receive formal education in entrepreneurship. So, what is wrong? I am not sure there is something wrong with entrepreneurship education in general, except too much trust in theoretical, readily applicable and scholastic knowledge.

It is possible that this kind of theoretical and applicable technology (although hermeneutic in principle) is its ability to close off other forms of education and pedagogies. It is not the case that even the idea of other forms of disclosure being possible is negated, but they are certainly mute and therefore not applicable and not in use. Maybe this is due to the sharp focus on how Beings should present themselves only in terms of their utility and effectiveness.

Although traditional learning focuses on what is (Heidegger 1968), it may be far more illuminating to examine the boundaries of ordinary knowledge by trying to study what is not. Here, I ask for the possibility for nothing in (entrepreneurial) higher education. This leads us towards a thinking that there is an activity (or passivity; cf. 2.3) that occurs beneath the surface and indeed is not grasped by theoretical or scholastic knowledge. Is this possible, i.e. to let students learn or allow the student to dwell in a mode that privileges absence? This means not just a focus on what appears before the student and teacher, but on considering whether it appears at all and the context framing appearances when they occur.

Even though Heidegger develops this (fundamental) ontology as an account of the human being, and definitely not as a method of enquiry for students or as a pedagogical tool, it also has its "effect" on pedagogy and teaching practice. Two of Heidegger's leading concepts are introduced below. Together they are sufficient to sketch a Heideggerian concept of (nothing) pedagogy, one specifically drawn for teachers. There are two concepts that are central to Heidegger and that are relevant in the construction of a hermeneutic Nothing pedagogy. These concepts are (1) Being-in-the-world/thrownness and (2) listening/passivity

This pedagogy is consistent with Heidegger's 1951–1952 account of teaching and learning:

> Teaching is even more difficult than learning. We know that; but we rarely think about it. And why is teaching more difficult than learning? Not because the teacher must have a larger store of information, and have it always ready. Teaching is more difficult than learning because what teaching calls for is this: to let learn. The real teacher, in fact, lets nothing else be learned than—learning. His conduct, therefore, often produces the impression that we properly learn nothing from him, if by "learning" we now suddenly understand merely the procurement of useful information. The teacher is ahead of his apprentices in this alone, that he has still far more to learn than they—he has to learn to let them learn.
>
> (Heidegger 1968, p. 15)

Being-in-the-World

This is apparent in the way that the teacher urges students to enquire and dwell in the "personal" or "individual" aspects of situations. For example, in thinking about business the notion of "profit" often arises. This could be pursued in the manner of Wittgenstein (in his work on conceptual analysis with the example of "games"); it would be possible to ask about the use of the word "profit", network, partners, customer, market, risk, uncertainty, success, failure, trust, in different contexts and by different business people. Drawing upon Wittgenstein's discussion of chess (for example), we could urge students to determine the rules of the game of business (para. 197, Wittgenstein 2001, p. 68). In response to this predicament, I might ask a Heideggerian question: What is the foundation of a situation where the concept of market is an issue?

So, the crucial question is: When in the present course study means contemplate, ponder or ruminate within the full situation as a being worlded. Furthermore, it is perhaps unhelpful for teachers or students to bring into discussions dichotomies such as school and home, work and leisure, public and private, because being-in-the-world could be less genuine. The slaying of dichotomies is a topic I shall return to shortly in the section on listening. The relevance of this in the teaching of business analysis is that it opens doors to the student's engagement with course matters in a very full manner. No longer is the course a confined slice of a student's life. Business analysis is not abstract, unrelated to the student, scientific, objective, or purely intellectual. It is like business itself—something that takes over oneself. Accordingly, an important realization for students is that there is no separation between their personal situation and their business, work or school life.

Listening

Listening is about not refusing to know or understand. Listening (or hearing, as Heidegger 1968 would say) presupposes a greater form of openness: what is to be listened to has to do with a quality in communication about which comprehension is only graspable on the side of the *Same*, whereas the encounter summoning both teacher and student is the encounter with the *other*. Listening implies welcoming the teacher's speech without immediately reducing the latter to an assured "I hear you"; it implies allowing the alienness and potential nothingness that dwells in that speech to run its course, through the student's attempt to depose her own ego. The student's aural offering thus denotes a disposition in which attention cannot be exclusively paid to signifiers, insofar as the other's speech, received in a state of passivity (cf. 4.3), is to give way to felt experiences in the teacher (or other fellow students), leading to perceptible changes in their listening.

However, it is not the speech between teacher–students or students–students that is important here.

Heidegger provides a concept of discourse in section 34 of *Being and Time*. Heidegger (1978, p. 161) points out that discourse is the foundation of language (Heidegger 1978, p. 161). Discourse, and thus the relation to others whom we address (a kind of ontological addressivity), is the primordial phenomenon in comparison to verbal language. This challenge to the common understanding of language as concerned with conveying information comes about because we do not acknowledge that verbal language derives from discourse. This derivation includes gestures, mimics, sounds etc. However, Heidegger (1978) stresses that we never just hear sounds, but hear specific entities. We immediately give meaning to what we hear; we make sense and are affected by this sense. Especially in situations of teaching and learning, this relation needs to be considered. Thirdly, "hearing and keeping silent are possibilities belonging to discoursing speech" (Heidegger 1978, p. 161). Silence is not a lack of speech, but a genuine and very important dimension of discourse.

What does this mean for entrepreneurial education discourse? Discourse is certainly not limited to the words that are being spoken in the auditorium or learning situations. Leaping-ahead listening, for teachers, can consist in open-ended questions, nodding in support, supporting in the form of confirming body language if desired: being-with that goes beyond words. It is crucial for the teacher to *be there (dasein)*. Discourse which involves (verbal) silence, listening and letting-be allows the student to remain a "who", that is, own up to being and remain a "who" in the situation. It means supporting passivity rather than interrupting it, acknowledging the existential precariousness that makes even the most ordinary mundane problem suddenly complex, and listening to what the student needs, no matter how difficult it may be for her to convey it. Of course, the emphasis placed on silence in this respect is not meant as a categorical demand to be without words; teachers and students can also speak to reassure as well as to inform. Equally significant is the willingness to be silent and the understanding that a response from the teacher or the student should not always be expected.

To summarize in more poetic language: a heightened state of emotion, listening (as a form of expression) and the mysterious power of art (Nothing) to deeply move a person (researchers, students etc.). Nothing as listening surges up from the soles of the feet, a kind of permission to find or locate a voice, i.e. to locate a being who is struggling for its own existence. The Nothings oeuvre may be irrational, a heightened awareness and a dash of being. Nothing as the voice of shadow and listening. A kind of getting rid of the (cognitive) scaffolding and applied paradigm thinking (technology). Maybe the basic tone of Nothing is a gentle laugh sweeping you away and getting you to stop thinking, to stop analyzing and problem solving.

References

Gadamer, H. G. (2004). *Truth and Method*. London: Continuum International Publishing Group Ltd.

Heidegger, M. (1962). *Being and Time*. New York: Harper & Row Publishers.

Heidegger, M. (1968). *What is called thinking?* (F.D. Wieck & J.G. Gray, Trans.). New York, NY: Harper Collins.

Heidegger, M. (1978). *Poetry, Language, Thought*. New York: Harper Collins.

Hjorth, D. & Johannisson, B. (2009). Learning as an entrepreneurial process. *Revue de l'Entrepreneuriat*, 8(2), 57–78.

Lautenschlager, A. & Haase, H. (2011). The myth of entrepreneur-ship education: Seven arguments against teaching business creation at universities. *Journal of Entrepreneurship Education*, 14, 147–161.

MacDonald, P. S. (2000). *The Existential Reader*. Edinburgh: Edinburgh University Press.

March, J. G. & Simon, H. A. (1966). *Organizations*. Oxford: John Wiley and Sons.

Perren, L. & Ram, M. (2004). Case study method in small business and entrepreneurial research: Mapping boundaries and perspectives. *International Small Business Journal*, 22(1), 83–104.

Shane, S. A. (2003). *A General Theory of Entrepreneurship: The Individual-Opportunity Nexus*. Cheltenham: Edward Elgar Publishing.

Steeter, D. H., Kher, R. & Jacquette, J. (2011). University-wide trends in entrepreneurship education and the rankings: A dilemma. *Journal of Entrepreneurship Education*, 14, 75–92.

Vetrivel, S. C. (2011). Entrepreneurship and education: A missing key in development theory and practice. *Advances in Management*, 3, 18–22.

Vygotsky, L. S. (1978). *Mind in Society: The Development of Higher Psychological Process*. Cambridge, MA: Harvard University Press.

Wittgenstein, L. (2001). *Tractacus Logico Philosophicus*. London: Routledge.

7 Conclusion

Nothing as the Nascent and Revitalizing Entrepreneurship

Entrepreneurs show tendencies towards what Heidegger (1962) identifies as existence's inherent and preliminarily interpretive (hermeneutical) nature, that is to say, how entrepreneurs encounter opportunities, and how they grasp them and are owned and transformed by the opportunities in practice; in other words, the Theory of nothing-in-practice. When the entrepreneurship/Nothing awakens within the entrepreneur, it starts each time from the top again and the entrepreneurship is not shut down in a systematic way from within. It follows, therefore, that it is impossible to develop a systematic, unquestionable and finally rounded-off entrepreneurship for the entrepreneur. Entrepreneurship and its nature are a beginning. Adopting a Heideggerian Nothing philosophy, one can say that established (entrepreneurial) theoretical positions become parenthetical or are withdrawn (cf. 2.1–2.3).

Being-there is assigned the task of responding to one's own unique situation. The response to the opportunity of the situation can perhaps be understood here as a (naïve, solipsistic) withdrawal from the world—a withdrawal that leads to justifiably posing critical questions concerning the ethical and political implications of Heidegger's philosophy. Like Heidegger, Habermas (1984) also insists on regaining and enriching opportunities for (communicative) action, although the two disagree on the feasibility of formulating a normative basis for such acts. Habermas (1984) claims that Heidegger may be accused of abstracting away from societal and normative validity requirements. The criticism is raised based on a judgement that key terms such as Being-there (Dasein), truth (*Aletheia*) and Being-with (*Mit-sein*) prevent a necessary illumination of intersubjective and communicative factors in human activities. For Habermas (1984), it appears that Dasein disappears from society and real history and thus cannot take the responsibility to prevent a new Holocaust. In other words, in Habermas's view, Dasein does not necessarily pose the compelling question of what the thinking self is when it thinks, and this can lead to one thinking too highly of oneself and that the mind owns existence to an exaggerated extent. More specifically, episodes in Heidegger's own life might exemplify this "grandeur", or as Safranski (1998) says regarding Heidegger's relationship to National Socialism: "For It was not the discussion of national socialism, but the national socialist revolution itself—as he perceived it at the time—that to his mind meant a renewal" (p. 444). It is also rather doubtful that Heidegger's philosophy can be put in direct relationship with the ideology of National Socialism (Safranski 1998), but it seems obvious that Heidegger's philosophy could give impetus to a national socialist revolution. This is unacceptable for Habermas (1984), who seems to build his entire philosophical project on a fundamental distance from all the signs (and potentials) of modern crimes of the Holocaust type and from a modern will to enforcing a fascist/Nazi and totalitarian social order. For Heidegger (1962), it seems impossible to articulate a priori normative and political perspectives.

Based on Heidegger (1962), an intention is given that is different from formulating a normative basis for a political criticism; "We shall not and cannot fixate what at any given moment and in each individual case, in an existential sense, is called inside and within Dasein. . . . The situation is the 'there' that in each case is opened in determination" (pp. 261 and 280). It is the insight of Being-there that constitutes the situation (and not just a glance for the situation). Only when Being-there is brought into the situation can the opportunity be discovered. It is also possible to see that the content of the situation is not of particular importance, but rather how one relates to it. It is thus only the individual decisive glance of Being-there that can be sure of its content. This "general" emptiness of content emptiness can be criticized for not pointing out a direction or an object. Heidegger does not seem to want to propose an objectifying content or a predetermined object for Being-there/existence, perhaps because the objectivism-relativism dichotomy is considered false in a phenomenological perspective, which usually wants to go back to the phenomenon itself. The issue of objectivism-relativism does not affect what is essential for Heidegger (1962); namely that which is present before us or the actual life. This can be read as an entrepreneurial appeal that every Being-there/existence in their actual life (practical understanding) should see through themselves to be able to realize themselves. Entrepreneurship is thus entrusted to its own direction and its own object rooted in domestic terms that form the basis out of which we think and experience. The meaning of Being-there in one's actual life is closely associated with the question of meaning, oblivion and possibility of existence. The following is an example:

> The example is from the Taoist parable of Chuang-Tzu (paraphrased from Rojecewicz 2006, p. 230), where Tzu-Kung is speaking with an old wise man who is tending his garden. . . . The old man digs ditches in the irrigated garden and uses a pitcher to pour water over

into the ditches from the source wellspring. The labour is toilful and goes slowly for the old man. Tzu-Kung tells him of a contrivance that can make the work much more effective and less tiring. He tells the old man about the advantages of making an artificial wooden device that carries two buckets of water (lever principle), so that the work would be much easier and more efficient. The old wise man responded mockingly that he would be ashamed of having to use the wooden arm device, because those who use artificial things/machinery also perform work in a machine-like and artificial manner. Thus, the message is that machine-like work leads to a heartless and "stone-like" man who is no longer able to preserve sheer simplicity. And those who are without this simplicity are insecure in their exuberance and spirit/soul, which in turn is not in accordance with walking the path and reaching great truth. It is not a Heideggerian mindset to assume that those who perform work with machines become themselves machine-like in their existence (as if the absence of machinery and modern technology would be a guarantee of Dasein's realization of possibilities).

In an entrepreneurial (nothing) practice, even presenting itself one-sidedly with the aid of modern technology and machine-like contrivances (advanced analysis of markets, customers, potential partners and competitors using technology data tools/programmes used in a result-oriented practice), it is in principle not cut off from the realizations of existence and the enlightenment of Being.

In this respect, Heidegger (1962) can contribute to a deliberation concerning modernness: whether any system/practice that is so refined and well developed in its expression that it fails to see its own limitation; that it transcends itself and its own logic. This can be understood as an appeal for another entrepreneurship rather than the modern, with a progressive finality and a focus on technology/tools that never loses sight of the use of tools—a modern practice that is overly concerned with the aftermath, the result, and where nothing happens "there" after the tools are used and one forgets the question concerning the meaning of being. The whole thing simply depends on whether one is open to the question of being, that is, whether one is willing to sacrifice oneself for the open locus of Being. To be "there" like a recoil out in a clearing, to perceive oneself as being in a place where the world/practice takes notice that one is already there among the currents/technologies, denotes some of the question's necessarily blurred clarity and opening power. Safranski (1998) exemplifies this as follows:

> With the issue of Being, most people meet the same fate as the student in a Zen anecdote.

He had long pondered the problem of how one could get the grown goose out of the thin-necked bottle without killing the bird or breaking the bottle. The pupil, who had speculated with all his might about this, went to his master and asked for the solution to the problem. The master turned away for a moment, then clapped his hands and called the pupil by his name. "Here am I, master!", the pupil replied. "Do you see", said the master, "the goose is out!" So much for the question of the meaning of being.

(p. 453)

Perhaps, such an "awakening" denotes an opening and challenge to self-understanding. More specifically, one might ask whether an entrepreneurial practice (it also applies to researchers) often forgets the value of positioning oneself in relation to self-understanding, to position oneself in relation to one's own existence. This is also a question of remaining open to the mystery of Being, which for the entrepreneur means realizing existence anew and which on a general basis can be a nascent and revitalizing entrepreneurship. In other words, an entrepreneurship founded on Nothing. It is a matter only of putting the entrepreneur/researcher in motion in the centre of a world from which we have vanished to again awaken to ourselves.

References

Habermas, J. (1984). *The Philosophical Discourse of Modernity*. Cambridge: Polity.
Heidegger, M. (1962). *Being and Time*. New York: Harper & Row Publishers.
Rojecewicz, R. (2006). *The Gods and Technology*. New York: State University of New York Press.
Safranski, R. (1998). *En mester fra Tyskland. Heidegger og hans tid*. Oslo: Gyldendal.

Bibliography

Abernathy, W. J., & Clark, K. B. (1985). Innovation: Mapping the Winds of Creative Destruction. *Research Policy*, *14*(1), 3–22. https://doi.org/10.1016/0048-7333(85)90021-6

Almond, G. A., & Verba, S. (Eds.). (1963). *The Civic Culture Revisited*. Newbury Park: Sage Publications.

Anheier, H. K. (2014). *Nonprofit Organizations: Theory, Management, Policy* (expanded and revised 2nd ed.). Oxford, New York: Routledge.

Anheier, H. K., & Salamon, L. (Eds.). (1997). *Defining the Nonprofit Sector*. Manchester: Manchester University Press.

Archibugi, D., & Iammarino, S. (2002). The Globalization of Technological Innovation: Definition and Evidence. *Review of International Political Economy*, *9*(1), 98–122.

Ben-Ner, A., & van Hoomissen, T. (1991). Nonprofit Organizations in the Mixed Economy: A Demand and Supply Analysis. *Annals of Public and Cooperative Economics*, *4*, 519–550.

Christensen, C. M. (2000). *The Innovator's Dilemma: When New Technologies Cause Great Firms to Fail. The Management of Innovation and Change Series*. Boston, MA: Harvard Business School Press.

Collier, D. (2011). Understanding Process Tracing. *PS: Political Science & Politics*, *44*(4), 823–830. https://doi.org/10.1017/S1049096511001429

Crepaldi, C., Rosa, E. de, & Pesce, F. (2012). *Literature Review on Innovation in Social Services in Europe: Sectors of Health, Education and Welfare Services*. Report from Innoserv. http://www.solidar.org/system/downloads/attachments/000/000/106/original/final_report_wp1_-_literature_review-2.pdf?1457601223

Davies, B. P., & Knapp, M. (1994). Improving Equity and Efficiency in British Community Care. *Social Policy & Administration*, *28*(3), 263–285.

Drummond, M. F., Stoddart, G. L., & Torrance, G. W. (1998). *Methods for Economic Evaluation of Health Care Programmes* (2nd ed.). Oxford, New York, Toronto: Oxford University Press.

Eisenhardt, K. M. (1989). Building Theories from Case Study Research. *Academy of Management Review*, *14*(4), 532–550.

Fligstein, N., & McAdam, D. (2012). *A Theory of Fields*. Oxford, New York: Oxford University Press.

Flynn, P., & Hodgkinson, V. A. (2001). *Measuring the Impact of the Nonprofit Sector*. New York: Kluwer Academic, Plenum Publishers.

George, A. L., & Bennett, A. (2005). *Case Studies and Theory Development in the Social Science*. Cambridge: MIT Press.

Halman, L., & Nevitte, N. (1996). *Political Value Change in Western Democracies: Integration, Values, Identification, and Participation. European Values Studies*. Tilburg, The Netherlands: Tilburg University Press.

Hansmann, H. (1980). The Role of Nonprofit Enterprise. *The Yale Law Journal, 89*(8), 835–902.

Hansmann, H. (2006). Economic Theories of Non-Profit Organizations. In W. W. Powell & R. Steinberg (Eds.), *The Nonprofit Sector: A Research Handbook*. New Haven, London: Yale University Press.

Henderson, R. M., & Clark, K. B. (1990). Architectural Innovation: The Reconfiguration of Existing Product Technologies and the Failure of Established Firms. *Administrative Science Quarterly, 35*(1), 9–30. https://doi.org/10.2307/2393549

Kaplan, R. S. (2001). Strategic Performance Measurement and Management in Nonprofit Organizations. *Nonprofit Management and Leadership, 11*(3), 353–370. https://doi.org/10.1002/nml.11308

Kendall, J., & Knapp, M. (2000). Measuring the Performance of Voluntary Organizations. *Public Management Review, 2*(1), 105–132.

McCrone, P., & Knapp, M. (2007). Economic Evaluation of Early Intervention Services. *British Journal of Psychiatry, 191*(51), 19–22.

Nicholls, A., & Murdock, A. (Eds.). (2012). *Social Innovation: Blurring Boundaries to Reconfigure Markets*. Houndmills, Basingstoke, Hampshire, New York: Palgrave Macmillan.

Putnam, R. D. (2000). *Bowling Alone: The Collapse and Revival of American Community*. New York: Simon & Schuster.

Putnam, R. D., Leonardi, R., & Nanetti, R. (1993). *Making Democracy Work: Civic Traditions in Modern Italy*. Princeton, NJ: Princeton University Press.

Rosenbaum, M. S., Corus, C., Ostrom, A. L., Anderson, L., Fisk, R. P., Gallan, A. S., . . . Williams, J. D. (2011). Conceptualization and Aspirations of Transformative Service Research. *Journal of Research for Consumers, 19*, 1–6.

United Nations Statistical Division. (2003). *Handbook on Non-Profit Institutions in the System of National Accounts. Studies in Methods: Series F: Vol. 91*. New York: United Nations.

Weisbrod, B. A. (1975). Toward a Theory of the Voluntary Nonprofit Sector in a Three-Sector-Economy. In E. S. Phelps (Ed.), *Altruism, Morality, and Economic Theory* (pp. 171–195). New York, NY: Russell Sage Foundation.

Weisbrod, B. A. (1998). *To Profit or Not to Profit: The Commercial Transformation of the Nonprofit Sector*. Cambridge, New York, NY: Cambridge University Press.

Young, D. R., & Steinberg, R. (1995). *Economics for Nonprofit Managers*. New York: Foundation Center.

Young Foundation, The. (2012). *Social Innovation Overview, Part I: Defining Social Innovation*. A Deliverable to the Project "The Theoretical, Empirical and Policy Foundations for Building Social Innovation in Europe" (DG Research). Brussels.

Zapf, W. (1989). Über Soziale Innovationen. *Soziale Welt, 40*(1–2), 170–183.

Index

active/activity: passivity vs. 29–34; staged-venture creative 30
active entrepreneurship 32
active nothing 6, 8–9
alert entrepreneur 13
Amjadi, M. 15
Angle, H. 30
angst 49–51, 60–66
anxiety *see* angst
Apple 80–81
applicable paradigm 1–5, 57–60, 66–69, 90, 93; *see also* technology, nature of, tools
articulation potential of Nothing 7
Åsvoll, H. 15, 62
avoiding Nothingness 61–62

Bakhtin, M. 26, 76
becoming: being vs. 21–27; importance of dialogue in 24; prosaic research and 24–27
being: becoming vs. 21–27; nothing and 49; as subject/individual 27; trans-being 27; *see also* being-in-the-world, being-there (*Dasein*)
Being and Time (Heidegger) 43, 44, 48
being-in-the-world: entrepreneurs relying on 90; establishment of 43–44; Gadamer on 35; passivity and 35; teaching 95–96; as technology 46–48; terribleness as basic mode of 51–53
being-there (*Dasein*): definition of 44; distanced theoretical understanding and 45; establishment of 43; existential confrontation of 45;

Habermas on 99; hammer example 45; past actions influence on 91; practical understanding 45; as response to a situation 99–102; in terms of possibilities 54; time as meaning of 51–52
Berglund, H. 15
body language 97
Burmeister-Lamp, K. 27
business plans 2, 30, 57, 59, 78

Carter, N.M. 21–22
Cartesian theoretical mode 3–4, 33–34, 92–93
clock time 47
cognition research *see* entrepreneurial cognition
consciousness, development of 35
correspondence theories of truth 23–24, 87
creation activities 30
creative effectuation 4, 31
Critcley, S. 50
Crossan, M. 22

Dasein (being there/existence) *see* being-there (*Dasein*)
decision-making: dwelling vs. 27–29; examples of 27–28; problems reinforcing themselves in 93; side effects of 65–66; as theory 27; tool-based view of 28
decision-making knowledge 2–3, 28
decision theory 93
Dewey, J. 74
dialogical learning 89–90

Printed in the United States
by Baker & Taylor Publisher Services